EYEWITNE

ANIMAL

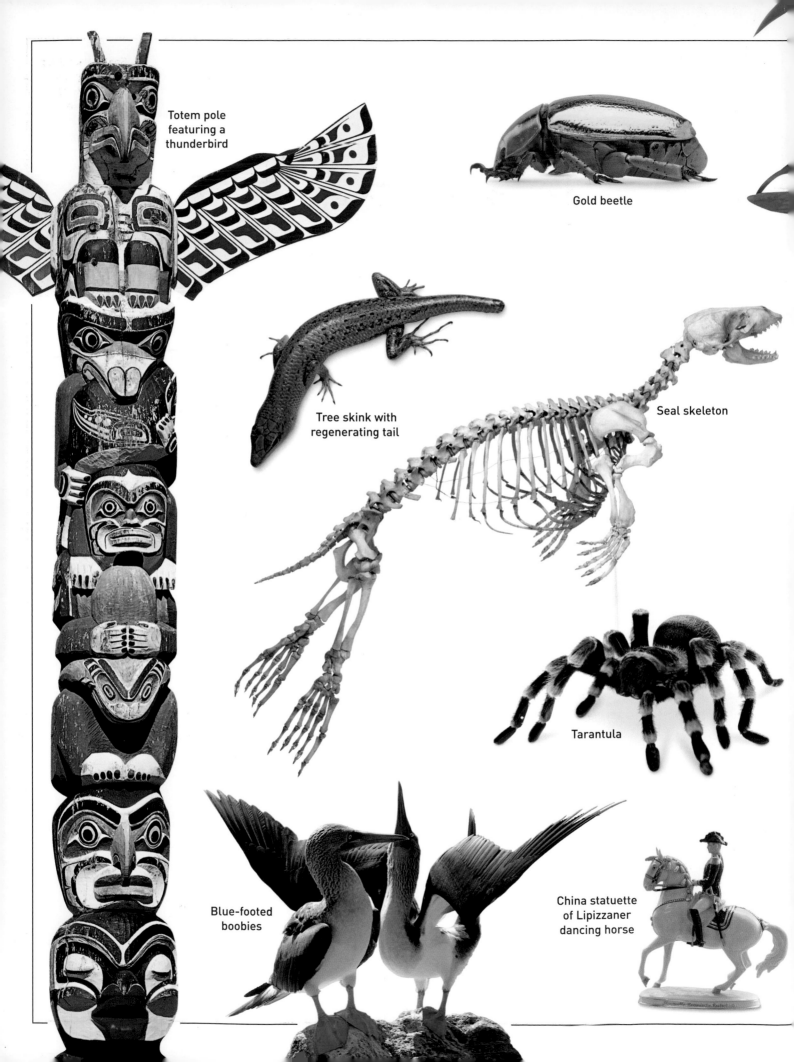

Totem pole featuring a thunderbird

Gold beetle

Tree skink with regenerating tail

Seal skeleton

Tarantula

Blue-footed boobies

China statuette of Lipizzaner dancing horse

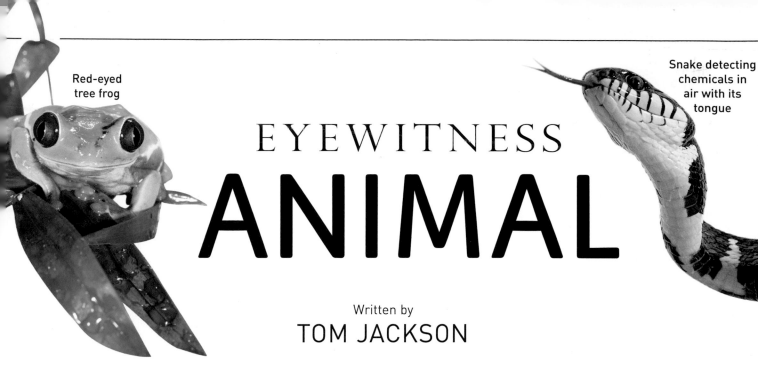

Red-eyed
tree frog

Snake detecting
chemicals in
air with its
tongue

EYEWITNESS
ANIMAL

Written by
TOM JACKSON

Common octopus

Fisher's lovebirds

European common frog

Hamster

Penguin and chick

Blue morpho butterfly

Homo habilis, a human ancestor

American cockroaches

Penguin Random House

Consultant Dr Kim Dennis-Bryan

DK Delhi
Project editor Bharti Bedi
Project art editor Deep Shikha Walia
Senior editor Kingshuk Ghoshal
Senior art editor Govind Mittal
Senior DTP designer Tarun Sharma
DTP designer Neeraj Bhatia
DTP manager Sunil Sharma
Deputy managing editor Eman Chowdhary
Managing art editor Romi Chakraborty
Production manager Pankaj Sharma
Jacket designer Govind Mittal

DK London
Senior editor Dr Rob Houston
Senior art editor Philip Letsu
Publisher Andrew Macintyre
Picture researcher Myriam Mégharbi
Production editor Ben Marcus
Production controller Luca Frassinetti

Relaunch Edition (DK UK)
Senior editor Chris Hawkes
Senior art editor Spencer Holbrook
Jacket editor Claire Gell
Jacket designer Laura Brim
Jacket design development manager Sophia MTT
Producer, pre-production Francesca Wardell
Producer Janis Griffith
Managing editor Linda Esposito
Managing art editor Philip Letsu
Publisher Andrew Macintyre
Publishing director Jonathan Metcalf
Associate publishing director Liz Wheeler
Design director Stuart Jackman

Relaunch Edition (DK India)
Project editor Bharti Bedi
Project art editor Nishesh Batnagar
DTP designer Pawan Kumar
Senior DTP designer Harish Aggarwal
Picture researcher Nishwan Rasool
Jacket designer Dhirendra Singh
Managing jackets editor Saloni Talwar
Pre-production manager Balwant Singh
Managing editor Kingshuk Ghoshal
Managing art editor Govind Mittal

First published in Great Britain in 2012
This revised edition published in Great Britain in 2015
by Dorling Kindersley Limited,
80 Strand, London WC2R ORL

Discover more at
www.dk.com

Contents

What is an animal?

To date, only about 1.3 million of Earth's animal species have been identified. They range from tigers to dust mites, and even sea anemones and sponges. Each is made up of millions, if not billions, of cells, performing specialized jobs in the body. What sets animals apart from other many-celled organisms is that they are more mobile and survive by eating other life forms.

Belonging to a species
Every animal belongs to a species, the members of which look similar, and share the same lifestyle and habitats. Members of a species can breed and produce young. The colour, size, and body shape of this emerald tree boa help experts identify it.

Animal cell
All living bodies are formed of tiny units called cells. An animal cell is surrounded by a membrane made from a thin sheet of oily material. The flexible sheet can take any shape. Cells contain structures called organelles, which form their factories, power supply, and chemical transport system.

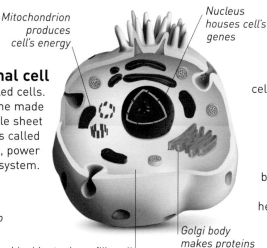

Mitochondrion produces cell's energy

Nucleus houses cell's genes

Golgi body makes proteins

Liquid cytoplasm fills cell

Going mobile
Animals are the only multicellular organisms (made from more than one cell) that can move from place to place. Most plants are rooted to something. Locomotion is usually as a response to changes in the environment. It is possible because an animal does not have rigid body cells. This helps it alter its body shape, so it can push against the ground or water to move.

Line of symmetry divides animal into equal halves

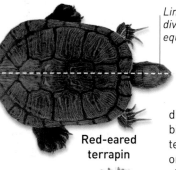

Red-eared terrapin

Line that divides animal into equal halves

Green sea anemone

Development plan
Every animal grows from a single cell that divides repeatedly, developing a body made of billions of cells. Most animals, such as this terrapin, develop bilaterally, with a mouth at one end and a rear opening at the other. Some simple animals, such as anemones, develop outwards from a central point.

Inside the animal kingdom
The system of organizing life into groups was developed by the Swede Carl Linnaeus in the 1750s. He split the animal kingdom into sub-groups based on their shared features. Phylum is the largest sub-group, followed by class, order, family, genus, and then species. Every animal has a unique scientific name, formed by its genus and species.

Classification of some salamander species

Chordata			(Phylum)
Vertebrata			(Sub-phylum)
Amphibia			(Class)
(Order)	Caudata	Anura	Gymnophiona
(Family)	Cryptobranchidae	Ambystomatidae / Plethodontidae	Sirenidae
(Genus)		*Plethodon*	
(Species)	*jordani*	*cinereus*	*glutinosus*

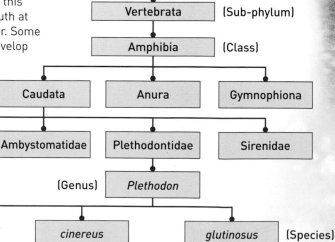

Plethodon jordani

Plethodon cinereus

Plethodon glutinosus

Ear and other sense organs give tiger information about its surroundings

Bamboo is low in nutrients, so giant pandas spend 16 hours a day eating

Eating food

Of all the multicellular life forms – plants, fungi, and animals – only animals eat. An animal eats food through its mouth. The body then extracts the nutrients it needs – the body's fuels and building materials – from the food, and expels the rest as dung. In scientific terms, an animal is a "heterotroph" – it survives by consuming the bodies of other life forms. A fungus absorbs nutrients through its body, while a plant is powered by the energy in sunlight and absorbs raw materials from the ground.

Producers	Primary consumers	Secondary consumers	Tertiary consumers	Quaternary consumers

PHYTOPLANKTON · KRILL · WHALE · ALBATROSS · ARROW WORM · RADIOLARIAN · LEOPARD SEAL · PENGUIN · BLUE-GREEN BACTERIA · PELAGIC FISH · SQUID · DOLPHIN · COPEPOD · SEAWEED · MARINE WORM · BOTTOM-FEEDING FISH · KILLER WHALE

Webs of food

Living things in any environment are interconnected in food webs that link everything edible. It begins with producers, such as plants and bacteria – organisms that make their own food using energy from sunlight. Energy is then transferred to the primary consumers that feed on the producers, and so on.

Legs allow tiger to cross many different types of land surfaces efficiently

Almost an animal

Perhaps the closest life forms to animals are a selection of microscopic, single-celled organisms, including amoebae. These organisms can surround their tiny prey, such as algae, until it is completely engulfed.

Invertebrates

An invertebrate is an animal without vertebrae, or spine bones. These were the first animals on Earth, appearing in the oceans at least 700 million years ago. More than 95 per cent of animals alive today are invertebrates. There are more than 20 different groups, ranging from insects to jellyfish.

Head is smallest body section

Eye

Antenna

Thorax is middle body section

Jewel beetle

Hind wing

Wing case protects hind wing

Abdomen

As simple as it gets
Today's sponges may be similar to the first invertebrates. Their simple bodies are made up of just a handful of cell types. Pore cells let water into the body, and cone cells sieve food from it. Other cell types build the protein skeleton, including the spikes the sponge uses to fend off attack.

Blooming animals
Sea anemones are often mistaken for plants and are even named after a type of flower, but they are carnivorous animals. Anemones, jellyfish, and several other invertebrates have circular bodies, with no head at all.

Stinging tentacles look like petals

Segment joins with others to make up leg

In sections
All arthropods have a body that is divided into segments. In insects – the world's biggest animal group with 1 million species – however, some segments have fused (joined) together during evolution to form body sections. Insect bodies are built in three main parts – the head, thorax, and abdomen.

Many molluscs
The second largest invertebrate group are the molluscs, with 100,000 species. All mollusc bodies have one muscular "foot" to move, and the organs are held inside a mantle (a fleshy hood). Most molluscs have a hard shell made with a chalky mineral called calcium carbonate. Snails are some of the most common land molluscs. Several types, such as sea slugs and cephalopods, live without a shell.

Waterproof shell keeps body moist

Striped land snail

Mantle changes colour to blend in with surroundings

Tentacle lined with suckers

Many-footed head
The largest invertebrates are the cephalopods – a group of molluscs that includes octopuses, squid, and cuttlefish. Most of the body is the bulging mantle, while the foot is divided into flexible tentacles covered in suckers. Octopuses have eight, while other cephalopods have up to 90.

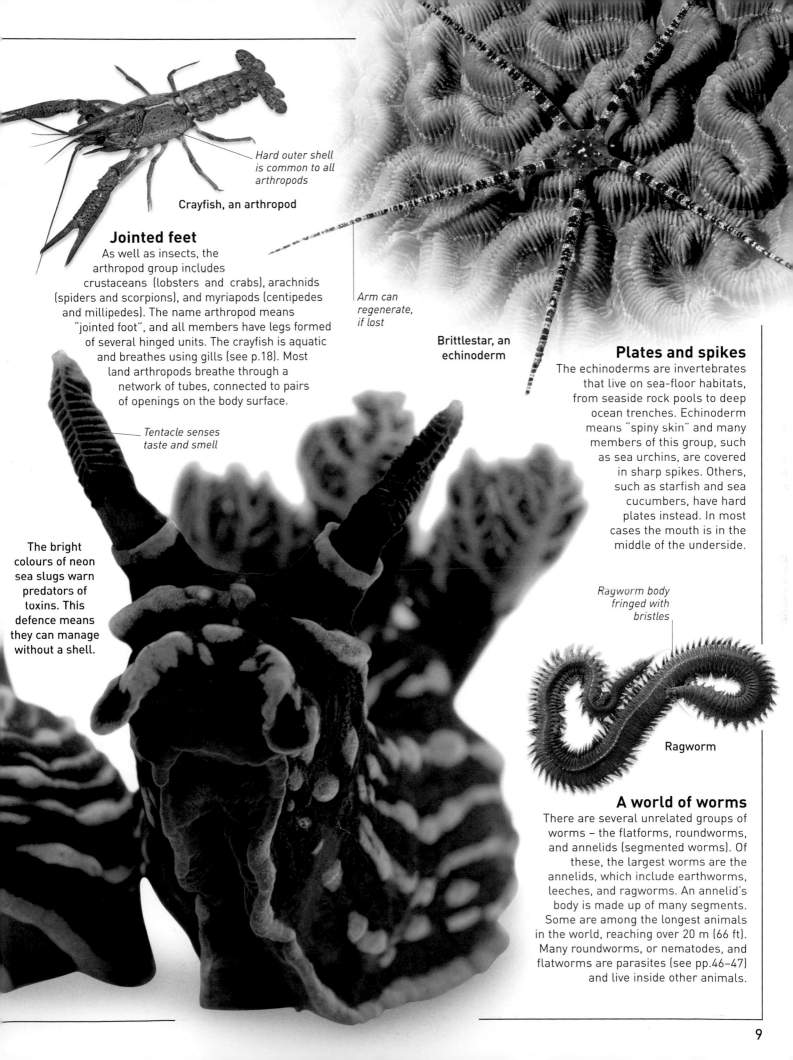

Hard outer shell is common to all arthropods

Crayfish, an arthropod

Jointed feet

As well as insects, the arthropod group includes crustaceans (lobsters and crabs), arachnids (spiders and scorpions), and myriapods (centipedes and millipedes). The name arthropod means "jointed foot", and all members have legs formed of several hinged units. The crayfish is aquatic and breathes using gills (see p.18). Most land arthropods breathe through a network of tubes, connected to pairs of openings on the body surface.

Arm can regenerate, if lost

Brittlestar, an echinoderm

Plates and spikes

The echinoderms are invertebrates that live on sea-floor habitats, from seaside rock pools to deep ocean trenches. Echinoderm means "spiny skin" and many members of this group, such as sea urchins, are covered in sharp spikes. Others, such as starfish and sea cucumbers, have hard plates instead. In most cases the mouth is in the middle of the underside.

Tentacle senses taste and smell

The bright colours of neon sea slugs warn predators of toxins. This defence means they can manage without a shell.

Ragworm body fringed with bristles

Ragworm

A world of worms

There are several unrelated groups of worms – the flatforms, roundworms, and annelids (segmented worms). Of these, the largest worms are the annelids, which include earthworms, leeches, and ragworms. An annelid's body is made up of many segments. Some are among the longest animals in the world, reaching over 20 m (66 ft). Many roundworms, or nematodes, and flatworms are parasites (see pp.46–47) and live inside other animals.

Cold-blooded vertebrates

The vertebrates are animals with a chain of bony segments running down the middle of their backs, forming a backbone. Each spine bone is called a vertebra. Fish, amphibians, and reptiles are all ectothermic, or "cold-blooded", vertebrates. Ectotherms cannot maintain a constant body temperature and rely on their surroundings to keep them warm.

Eardrum on the outside of head

Throat pouch puffed out to make calls

Moist skin lets oxygen and water through

Not a vertebrate

The lancelet is not a vertebrate since it has only a stiff cord supporting its back. With no skull, limbs, or side fins, it lives in the sea and grows to about the length of a finger. Biologists believe that vertebrates evolved from animals like the lancelet, about 530 million years ago.

Without jaws

Most vertebrates have jaws. However, this lamprey is jawless. It cannot bite its food. Instead, it twists its eel-like body to dig its spiral of teeth into the flesh of prey, or to scrape food from rocks.

Tail carries a venomous sting

Without bone

A vertebrate's body gets its shape from its internal skeleton. In most cases, the skeleton is made of hard, mineralized bone. However, sharks, skates, and these stingrays have bones built of cartilage, which is made from flexible protein.

Rays of bone

Most fish have ray fins formed from skin stretched over slim shafts of bone. Ray fins are ideal for wafting water, but are too weak to hold a fish's weight. Land vertebrates evolved from another group called lobe-finned fish, which have fleshy fins and thick bones.

Large thigh muscle powers jump

Long leg bones lever frog forwards

Spring king

Amphibians were the first land vertebrates. They are the ancestors of all tetrapods – animals with four limbs – including those with wings. Although, early tetrapods also had short, rigid necks, they looked nothing like modern frogs. With their very long back legs, frogs are built to jump.

Pectoral fin used for fine control

Tail fin used for propulsion

Webbed feet to aid swimming

Frilly gill absorbs oxygen from water

Life without legs

Not having legs makes it easier for snakes to slide through narrow burrows, twist and turn through tree branches, and slither over loose sand. Strong species, such as this cobra, can even rise up to stare into the eyes of taller animals. Snakes evolved from animals with legs. Some snake skeletons have hip bones where legs once attached to the body, and anacondas still have two tiny clawlike legs.

Between two worlds

Most amphibians live two lives. They start out in water, hatching from eggs laid in pools. They breathe with gills and swim with fins – like a fish. As they grow, amphibians develop legs for moving on land and switch to lungs for breathing. However, some species mix both ways of life. This mudpuppy stays underwater its whole life, but uses its legs to walk along river and stream beds.

High and dry

The reptiles were the first vertebrates to adopt a life away from water. They have waterproof scales to stop them drying out, and their eggs have a hard shell. Reptiles are cold-blooded and cannot heat their own bodies, so most live in warm parts of the world and must spend time basking in the sunlight.

Pectoral fin flaps like a wing to move ray forwards

Warm-blooded vertebrates

Birds and mammals are the only endothermic, or "warm-blooded", animals. Endothermic means "heat within". Endotherms can regulate their body temperature and keep warmer than their surroundings using fur, fat, or feathers to trap heat. Because of temperature controls, such as sweating, their body works well in most environments.

Flexible feathers

A bird's plumage, or covering of feathers, has several functions. Fluffy down feathers close to the skin trap air, creating a blanket of warm air around the body. The long, stiff, and very light feathers are used for flight. These coloured feathers also camouflage the bird and – for this macaw – attract mates.

Flight surface formed from overlapping feathers

Quill has tiny barbs that make it painful to pull out when stuck in skin

Flightless

The kiwi lives in New Zealand. Until humans arrived 750 years ago, it had no mammal predators, such as cats. The kiwi had no need to fly and did not develop a breastbone that could support strong flight muscles – making it a member of the flightless birds.

Feather vs hair

Hair and feathers are made of a waxy protein called keratin, which grows out of the skin in strands. Mammal hairs are of different lengths. The short underfur insulates, while longer guard hairs keep water and dirt out. Feathers are more complex – the strands branch out from a central shaft, before dividing again to form thin fibres that hook together to make a flat surface.

Flight feather extends back from bone at front of wing

Electron micrograph of fox fur (false colour)

Electron micrograph of feather (false colour)

Spikes and tufts

Mammal hair is sometimes put to unusual uses. For example, the defensive spikes, or quills, of a porcupine are very thick hairs. When threatened, a porcupine raises its quills, making itself appear larger than it is. Most of the quills point backwards, so if a predator attacks from behind, it gets a sharp shock. Other animals use their hair to communicate. Bushy-tailed squirrels signal to each other by flicking their fluffy tails.

Porcupine quills

Lumbar vertebra
(back bone)

Cranium
(skull)

Cervical
vertebra
(neck bone)

Mandible
(jawbone)

Rib

Caudal
vertebra
(tail bone)

**Skeleton
of grey
wolf**

Caudal vertebra
(tail bone)

Phalanx
(toe bone)

Ulna

Radius

Lumbar
vertebra
(back bone)

Cervical
vertebra
(neck bone)

Cranium
(skull)

Mandible
(jawbone)

Rib

Ulna

Radius

**Skeleton of
harbour seal**

Phalanx
(toe bone)

One skeleton fits all

The mammals are a diverse group. Wolves are built for a life on the run, while seals are only truly at home in the water. However, all mammals have the same set of bones. Both wolves and seals have seven neck vertebrae – the same as that of a human or a giraffe. The seal's flippers are merely longer, flatter versions of the wolf's springlike feet.

Laying eggs

Today, most mammals give birth to live young. The placentals nurture young inside their bodies (with a placenta), while marsupials give birth to immature young and nurture them inside a pouch. The duck-billed platypus does not belong to either group. When it was first discovered, scientists were surprised to find that it laid eggs. The platypus is one of five egg-laying mammal species, which belong to the group called monotremes.

Long,
coloured
tail feather

Forward-facing
eye

Primates

This mandrill is a primate. The primates are placental mammals, and include monkeys, lemurs, apes, and humans. Primates are one of the most widespread mammal groups. They evolved in the treetops, and their big brains, long limbs, and grasping hands were useful for life in the branches. Forward-facing eyes provide binocular vision for judging distances.

Orca, or killer
whale, breaches
surface of water

Mammals in water

Several mammal groups have evolved to survive in the water. Some, such as sea lions, still spend time on land, but the cetaceans (whales and dolphins) never set foot on shore. They have flippers in place of forelegs and no hind limbs at all. Cetaceans include dolphins, orcas, and the largest living animal – the blue whale.

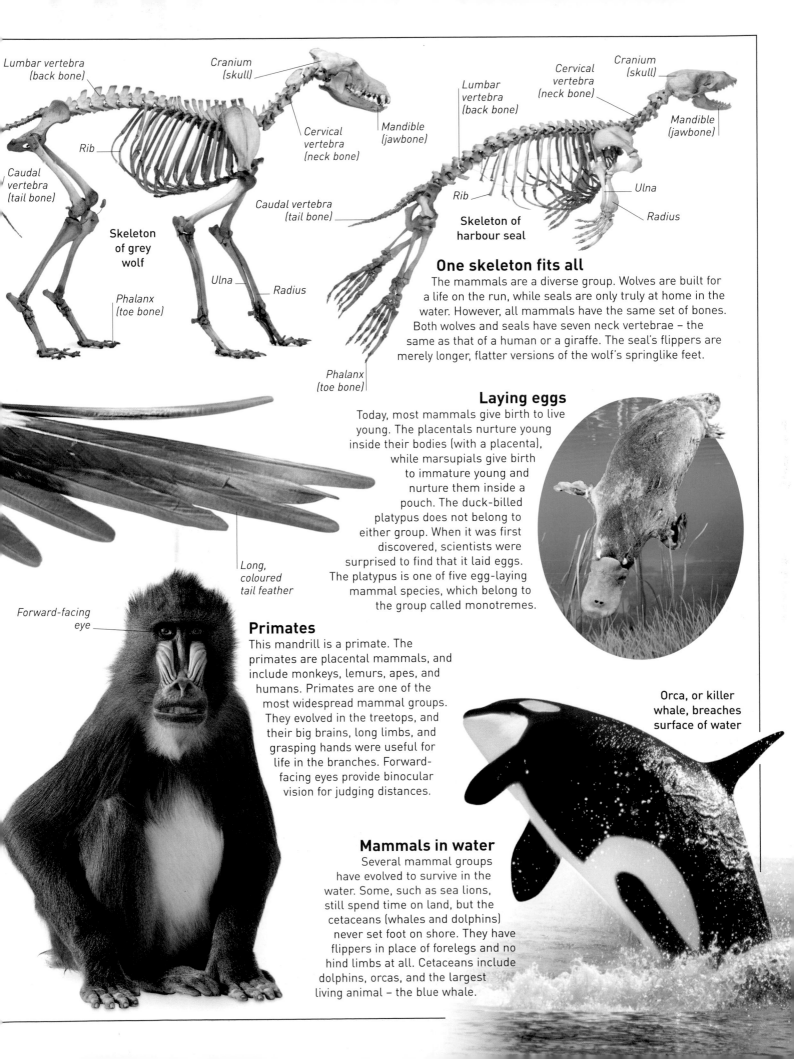

Evolution

Every species seems to be a perfect fit for its way of life. A sea snake has a flat, paddle-shaped tail that helps it swim, while a burrowing snake has a shovel-shaped snout suited to digging through soil. But both snakes have changed over time, evolving adaptations that better shape them to their environments. The driving force of this process is called natural selection.

Inherited features

The instructions for making a body are coded in an animal's genes – a set of chemicals called deoxyribonucleic acid (DNA) held in every cell. Genes are passed from parents to offspring and give the young traits of its parents – and an advantage (or disadvantage) over others. Those with desirable genes do well and have many offspring. As a result, their DNA becomes more common.

Thymine (T)

Guanine (G)

Adenine (A)

Cytosine (C)

Genes are strands of DNA coded with the chemical units, or bases, A, C, T, and G.

The backbone of DNA is made of sugar molecules

Long, toothy snout

Hind limb bones connect to the pelvis (hip bones)

Tall back bones anchor strong neck muscles

Hoofed foot

Wolf-like *Pakicetus* evolved around 55 million years ago. It had hoofed feet but was a hunter that caught fish.

Powerful tail helps animal swim

Crocodile-like *Ambulocetus* lived 50 million years ago.

Legs used to swim and walk on land

Webbed foot

Jawbone picks up sounds like a modern whale

Extended body

Blind progress

Evolution is happening all the time. The process has no direction – an animal can even reverse its path. For example, mammals evolved from animals whose ancestors were fish. Much later, some mammals began pursuing a watery lifestyle. Their legs slowly evolved into flippers and their bodies became fish-shaped. The result was today's whales.

Nostril halfway along snout

Hind limb is a small flipper

Bones of hind limb detached from pelvis

Dorudon lived in warm seas about 38 million years ago.

Large skull helps to break Arctic ice

Tail has become a paddlelike "fluke"

Balaena – the modern bowhead whale – gulps tiny krill with the largest mouth in the animal kingdom.

Tiny hind limb bones

Flipper

The father of evolution

In 1859, the English scientist Charles Darwin put forward the idea of evolution by natural selection in a book called *On the Origin of Species*. Much later, scientists found more evidence to back up the theory. Francis Crick and James Watson showed how DNA's coded genes are responsible for the inheritance of traits, which is a crucial mechanism for evolution.

Co-evolution

Sometimes, different organisms evolve together in a process called co-evolution. These acacia ants have co-evolved with the bullhorn acacia shrub – the ants make nests in the shrub's hollow thorns and sting anything that tries to eat its leaves. They also chew through invading creepers. In return, the acacia provides nectar and grows an edible fatty nodule.

Small, spiky thorn

Ants on patrol

Never the same

Natural selection exists because no two animals are the same. Even members of the same species are at least slightly different because they have a unique set of genes. These two ladybirds belong to the same species. Despite their noticeable warning patterns, a bird may eat one of the bugs. The other may survive and live to produce offspring.

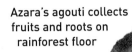

Azara's agouti collects fruits and roots on rainforest floor

The grey squirrel harvests nuts from trees

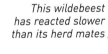

The Arabian spiny mouse forages for seeds in grasses

Radiating species

These rodents evolved from a single ancestor that lived 65 million years ago, but the different descendants have evolved in different directions. This "adaptive radiation" gives rise to a whole range of new species that live in different habitats but share features, such as gnawing front teeth.

This wildebeest has reacted slower than its herd mates

Survival of the fittest

Darwin described animals that were able to survive and reproduce as being "fit". In these terms, a fit animal is not just strong and healthy, its behaviour also makes it successful at surviving and reproducing. This cheetah is "fit" because it has got within pouncing distance of a wildebeest.

Extinct animals

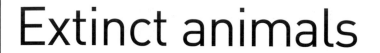

It is amazing to think that 99 per cent of all species that have ever lived on Earth are extinct. Over the last 700 million years, the animal kingdom has constantly changed, with new species taking the place of older ones. Extinction is a natural process. Animals may become extinct due to disasters. Species also die out when remaining members fail to reproduce, or when a new species evolves and is more successful in the struggle for survival.

Echmatocrinus, a primitive echinoderm

An explosion of life

A great blooming of species – called the Cambrian Explosion – happened around 530 million years ago (mya). Almost all animals living today – from fish to fleas – had an ancestor that once swam in the ocean during this period. All of the Cambrian species, including the invertebrates seen here, are now extinct, but they paved the way for the animal diversity we see today.

Studying fossils

Everything we know about extinct animals comes from fossils, which are the remains of animals, their footprints, and droppings, preserved in rocks. It is rare for whole skeletons to be preserved – palaeontologists (fossil scientists) build up a picture of how the animal looked and lived from fragments of bone. The large eye of this extinct sea reptile shows that it dived into dark waters.

Opabinia (possibly a giant ancestor of a tardigrade)

Haikouichthys, one of the earliest vertebrates

Marrella (thought to be a primitive arthropod)

Mass extinctions

Extinctions may occur due to a global catastrophe that kills thousands of species at once. Earth has witnessed at least five mass extinctions, the last of which occurred 65 mya when the dinosaurs died out. The worst extinction of all was the one around 250 mya, which wiped out most life on Earth.

Extinct humans

Our species, *Homo sapiens*, is not the first human species, but it is the only one that has not died out. One of the earliest members was *Homo habilis*, or "handy man", which lived between 2.3 and 1.4 mya. The last one to become extinct was the tiny "Flores man" – *Homo floresiensis* – which died out about 17,000 years ago.

Homo habilis made cutting tools out of flakes of stone

Corythosaurus, a dinosaur

Armour plates on a trilobite's back allowed it to roll up for protection

Dead end

An extinct species often leaves behind sister species, but some extinctions spell the end for an entire group of animals. Trilobites were one of the most common animals in the sea before they were all wiped out in the mass extinction around 250 mya.

Killed by humans

The thylacine, or marsupial tiger, became extinct in 1936 when the last one died in an Australian zoo. By then, all wild thylacines – predators more closely related to kangaroos than cats – had been shot, as they were considered pests. Humans have wiped out hundreds of species, from the Cuban coney to the dodo – often by accident.

Anomalocaris, a primitive arthropod

Wiwaxia, a primitive annelid

Hallucigenia (possibly a velvet worm)

Body systems

Just like a machine, an animal's body must be supplied with fuel and raw materials. It must also get rid of waste and repair itself when damaged. To carry out these functions most animals have a basic set of body systems, which each manage one set of life processes – digesting food, transporting nutrients and waste, moving, and protecting the body. Different animal bodies perform the same jobs in different ways.

Skeletons

Rigid skeletons provide a framework for an animal's body. For land animals, this allows them to raise their body parts against the pull of gravity. It also provides anchor points for muscles to pull on, allowing animals to move their bodies about. A vertebrate has an internal skeleton, but an insect, such as this beetle, has a hard exoskeleton (skeleton outside the body).

Hard wing case covers back

The flow of blood

Without a supply of blood and the oxygen it contains, an animal's body parts would soon start to die. As well as cells carrying oxygen, blood carries a range of chemicals. These include hormones – chemical messengers that control different body systems. For many animals, like this glass frog, blood travels inside special vessels that form the main chemical transport network. However, in invertebrates the blood sloshes through the whole body.

Heart pumps blood around body

Crab spider drinks fleshy soup

Meat soup

Usually, after swallowing food, an animal must digest it, to break it down into sugars, fats, and proteins. It then uses these substances as fuel or to build up the body. Digestion is mostly done by powerful chemicals in the stomach and intestines called enzymes. A spider, however, pumps its stomach enzymes into its prey, turning the victim's insides into a fleshy soup, which it then sucks up.

Pouch is full of water so gills work even above water level

Gas exchange

Animals take in oxygen and give out carbon dioxide in a process called gas exchange. Oxygen chemically breaks down sugar, releasing energy, and producing carbon dioxide as waste. Simple animals exchange gases through the surface of their bodies, but larger ones, like this mudskipper, use more complex systems like lungs and gills.

Body organs seen through the belly of a glass frog

Brain chain

The body's main communication system is made up of nerves, which work like wires carrying electric signals. The nerves connect to ganglion "junction boxes", which take care of different body sections. Vertebrates have a centralized nervous system under the control of a brain, while insects, such as this cockroach, have a chain of nearly independent ganglia.

Nerve connects to muscle

Single ganglion controls body part

Body shortens when longitudinal muscles contract

Leech pulled into a ball

Circular muscles contract to lengthen body

Leech extends its head

Body flattens as longitudinal muscles relax

Sucker anchors body

Body is fully stretched

Pull and stretch

Animals move using muscles, which are built up from tiny fibres made of two types of protein – actin and myosin. When muscles receive an electric pulse from a nerve, they shorten, for example drawing this leach into a ball. Muscles cannot push, so they work in pairs, in which one set produces the opposite movement to the other.

See-through skin on belly

Vein returns blood to heart

Blue skin warns that this frog is poisonous

Stripes hide a tiger in dry grasses

Clever skin

Skin is a tough but highly sensitive barrier, alerting an animal to cold, heat, and the slightest touch. It is also a self-repairing structure that acts as the first line of defence against diseases. Skin takes many forms, ranging from waterproof reptile scales, breathable amphibian skin, to the hair- and feather-covered skin of birds and mammals.

Crocodile scales have armoured bone plates

Bright parrot plumage attracts mates

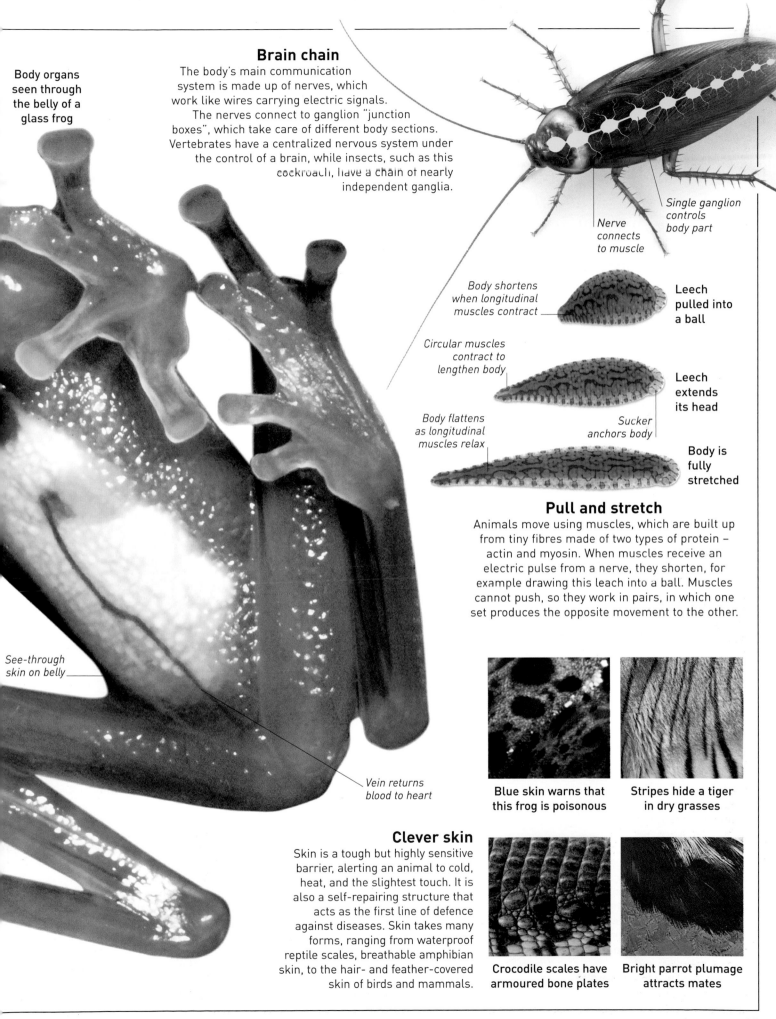

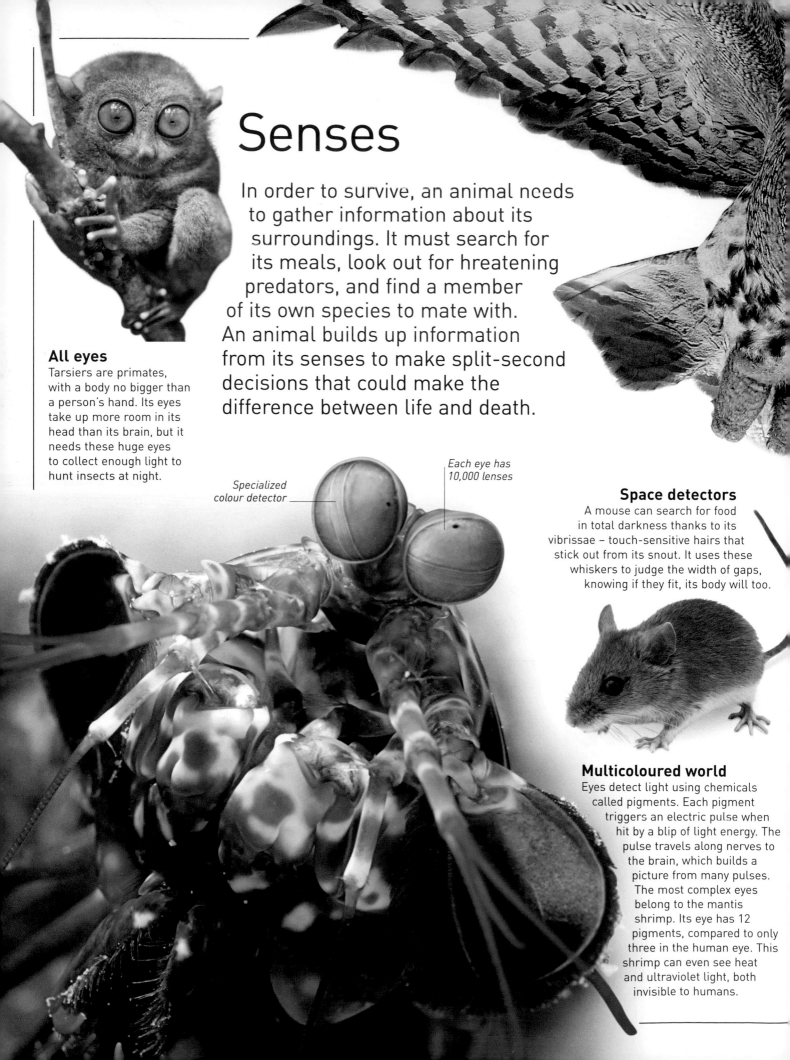

Senses

In order to survive, an animal needs to gather information about its surroundings. It must search for its meals, look out for hreatening predators, and find a member of its own species to mate with. An animal builds up information from its senses to make split-second decisions that could make the difference between life and death.

All eyes
Tarsiers are primates, with a body no bigger than a person's hand. Its eyes take up more room in its head than its brain, but it needs these huge eyes to collect enough light to hunt insects at night.

Specialized colour detector

Each eye has 10,000 lenses

Space detectors
A mouse can search for food in total darkness thanks to its vibrissae – touch-sensitive hairs that stick out from its snout. It uses these whiskers to judge the width of gaps, knowing if they fit, its body will too.

Multicoloured world
Eyes detect light using chemicals called pigments. Each pigment triggers an electric pulse when hit by a blip of light energy. The pulse travels along nerves to the brain, which builds a picture from many pulses. The most complex eyes belong to the mantis shrimp. Its eye has 12 pigments, compared to only three in the human eye. This shrimp can even see heat and ultraviolet light, both invisible to humans.

Dish face

An owl is a silent hunter. Its wings make no noise as it swoops in for a kill. The owl targets its prey carefully: it collects faint sounds using the disc of feathers around the face, which works like a satellite dish. The facial disc focuses the sound into the owl's ears beneath the feathers.

Prey

Jelly in ampulla converts electric signals into nerve pulses

Nerve carries pulses to brain

Faint electric field produced by fish's muscles

Scanner system

Sharks are sensitive to electric signals produced by their prey. Muscle movements generate weak electric fields that surround the shark's victims in the water. These signals are picked up by tiny pits, called ampullae of Lorenzini, dotted around the shark's snout. The ampullae even allow sharks to scan for prey buried in sand.

Feathery antenna traps chemicals floating in the air

Pointed tip of tongue collects scent chemicals in the air

Fire beetle and its detectors

Scent feelers

Antennae – the "feelers" on an invertebrate's head – are mostly used to feel objects. However, male moths use their feathery antennae to sweep the air for smells. The moth is most interested in picking up special scent chemicals released by females.

Tasting air

Most snakes rely on their smell senses to find food. As well as sniffing the air, a snake tastes it by flicking out its long forked tongue. It then slots the tips into a scent detector – Jacobson's organ – on the roof of its mouth. This organ detects which tip has more scent on it, and in which direction prey lies.

Hot spotters

Most animals get away from forest fires as fast as they can. However, a fire beetle heads straight for them: it is looking for recently burnt trees, in which to lay its wood-eating grubs. Its tiny heat sensors can pinpoint a fire from 12 km (7.5 miles) away.

Animal diets

Diet is a deciding factor in what an animal looks like and how it survives. Some species exploit one food source, while others survive on whatever comes their way. For instance, the snail kite is a little predatory bird that swoops over marshlands preying only on snails. In contrast, the Andean condor is an immense bird that glides for kilometres in search of a meal. It will eat anything, from the carcass of a beached whale to a nest full of eggs.

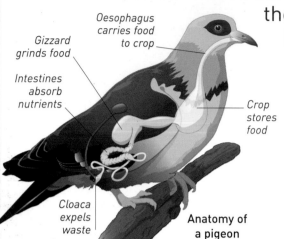

Oesophagus carries food to crop

Gizzard grinds food

Intestines absorb nutrients

Crop stores food

Cloaca expels waste

Anatomy of a pigeon

Long neck helps giraffe access food out of reach of most browsers

Digesting seeds
Many small birds, such as pigeons, are seed eaters. Seeds are packed with energy, but they have hard kernels. With no teeth, birds cannot chew. Instead, they grind the seeds in a muscular stomach pouch called the gizzard. Some birds peck grit to help grind the seeds more efficiently.

The ultimate browser
The giraffe is a browser – an animal that eats leaves. It strips away leaves, from even the prickliest trees, with its tough, long tongue. Browsers and grazers (animals that eat grasses) are herbivores and eat only plant food. Much of this diet is indigestible fibre and low in nutrients. Herbivores must feed constantly to keep their bodies supplied with energy. They also rely on stomach bacteria to break down some of the fibre into useful sugars.

Seek and destroy
Animals that eat nothing but meat are known as carnivores. This diet is very nutritious, as flesh is full of the proteins and fats needed to build a strong body. However, carnivores must use a lot of energy to catch prey. This lioness is chasing a kudu calf –even a predator as powerful as this fails to kill in six out of seven hunts.

Cooperative farmers

Leaf-cutter ants grow their own food. Worker ants use their slicing mouthparts to cut slabs of leaves. They carry them back to the nest and pile them up in deep "garden" chambers. A species of fungus grows on the rotting leaves, and that is what the adult ants eat and feed to their young. The ants tend their crops, controlling bacteria by applying pesticide chemicals in their saliva.

Acacia tree leaves cluster out of reach of most browsers

Dung ball from herbivore, such as cattle

Long back leg used to roll dung

Everything is food

Herbivores can only extract a small proportion of nutrients from their food, so their dung is a useful source of food for other animals. Dung beetles collect the waste and roll it into balls, inside which they lay their eggs – providing their grubs with a ready-made supply of dung to feast on.

Short head feathers do not get soaked with blood

Flesh of the dead

Animals that eat carrion – the flesh of dead animals – are called scavengers. A vulture is a top scavenger. It patrols the skies on wide wings and its hooked beak is ideal for ripping scraps of flesh from bones. The bird's stomach juices are highly acidic to kill any bacteria that may have infected the rotting carcasses.

Rüppell's vulture

Curiosity pays

Opportunist feeders never miss a chance to eat a meal. They are usually omnivores – animals that eat plant and animal food, dead or alive. The coati checks every nook and cranny with its long nose and sensitive forepaws. Its curiosity means it can find food almost anywhere – from a jungle to a junkyard.

Parenting

An animal that dies without reproducing cannot pass on its genes. In nature, the only animals that survive are those that are driven to reproduce. Most animals use sexual reproduction, in which a male and female pair up to mix both of their traits. This creates variation and increases the chances that some offspring will survive. After hatching or being born, young animals go through a period of growth.

Female   **Male**

Courting a mate

Strong and healthy animals make the best mates because it is likely that their offspring will be healthy too. The male blue-footed booby puts on a show for a potential mate by spreading his wings and stamping his feet. The deep blue colour of the feet are a sign that this male might make a good mate.

Changing sex

Sexual reproduction requires a male sex cell (sperm) to fuse with a female one (ovum, or egg). Generally, an animal is either male or female – it produces sex cells of only one kind. The bluehead wrasse does things differently. A young female lives with other females and a large, mature "supermale" with a bright blue head. When this male dies, the largest adult female in the group changes sex to become the next supermale.

Young female produces eggs

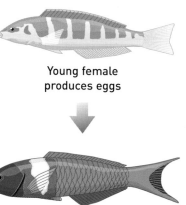

Supermale produces sperm instead of eggs

Precious cargo

An animal needs to ensure that its offspring survive long enough to reproduce themselves. Most invertebrates lay eggs in large numbers so that at least a few survive to adulthood. Scorpions, however, produce only a few eggs. The offspring spend the first part of their lives on their mother's back. The mother protects her newborns so that they have a better chance of growing up and breeding.

Mothered by father

Seahorses have a unique breeding system – the female produces the eggs and transfers them to a brood pouch on the male's belly. The eggs hatch inside the pouch, but the young, called fry, stay for a while longer, adapting to increasingly salty water.

Pouch holds around 200 fry

Starter home

Most mammal babies develop inside their mother's womb, or uterus, where a structure called the placenta supplies them with oxygen and food. However, marsupial mammals, such as this kangaroo, give birth to immature offspring. This young kangaroo (left), called a joey, was born blind and hairless, and its hind legs were just little lumps. With its clawlike arms, it heaved itself into its mother's pouch in which it will complete its development.

The cycle of life

A frog goes through several stages during its life. After hatching from eggs, the young – or larvae – begin to grow in water as tadpoles, froglets, and finally, frogs. As adults, a frog devotes its energy to finding a mate and producing eggs of its own. This takes place mainly on land. Since the adults are on land and larvae in water, they do not compete with each other for food.

Embryo in jelly

Frog spawn

Gills

Tail for swimming

Newly hatched tadpole

Half-tadpole, half-frog, 6–9 weeks

Tail slowly shrinks

Froglet emerges from water after about 12 weeks

Front legs now fully formed

Adult common frog

Female aphid giving birth to young

Mass production

Populations of aphids – also known as greenfly – grow very quickly using a form of asexual reproduction known as parthenogenesis. Females give birth to tiny clones (identical versions of themselves). These young aphids already have their own young developing inside them. In one summer as many as 40 generations can hatch. However, all the offspring share the weaknesses – susceptibility to disease, for example – of the parent. Therefore, in autumn, aphids lay eggs using sexual reproduction that ensure that a wide variety of individuals hatch out the following spring.

Caring parents

Most invertebrates and many fish produce many offspring and provide little parental care. Many mammals, however, have few young and devote a lot of time and energy to caring for them. Orangutans have one baby at a time, several years apart. The baby ape is almost helpless at birth. It also has a lot to learn – how to climb and where to find food – and needs its mother's help for its first five years or so.

Female orangutan with her babies

Marine animals

Life began in the oceans more than 3.5 billion years ago, and the oceans are still home to every major type of animal. However, the oceans are not a single habitat. Marine environments are as different as rocky shores, mangrove swamps, and deep ocean trenches. Biologists estimate that there is 300 times more living space in Earth's oceans than on dry land, and even in the open ocean there are variations in temperature, pressure, and saltiness that impact life.

Patrolling the shore
The shoreline is a crowded habitat. Here, the tides sweep regularly over the shore before receding. Being covered by sea water and then exposed to the air is difficult for coastal animals, and many of them hide out in mud when the tide recedes. These animals make a rich food source for waders, such as these red knots.

Coastal raiders
Many sea mammals and birds live on the coast but raid the water for food. Terns snatch fish, seals chase down squid, and diving otters collect shellfish. Sea otters have highly buoyant bodies, which is partly due to their thick fur. With 150,000 strands of hair per sq cm (1 million strands per sq in), it traps a lot of air – these hunters can even sleep while floating.

Underwater jungles
Corals are colonies of organisms that are tiny relatives of jellyfish. Each animal is called a polyp and grows a tiny protective case made from calcium carbonate, which is left behind when it dies. Generations of these skeletons build up into limestone reefs that can be several kilometres long. The complex shapes, holes, and crevices created by the coral skeletons provide a lot of different niches for animals, such as these yellow butterflyfish, to live in.

Schooling
There are few places to hide in the open ocean and some fish swim in clusters called schools, or shoals, to stay safe from predators. Each fish here is trying to get into the middle of a shoal where it is safer. They dart about, making it difficult for a predator to pick out a single target.

Spotted skin camouflages shark against sea bed

A docile shark
There are about 350 species of shark in the ocean. Some are fearsome, sharp-toothed predators that can prey on humans, but most sharks are harmless. This bullhead shark uses its sturdy fins to walk across the seabed at night, searching for urchins and crabs to feed on.

Mantle (body covering)

Fin flaps up and down to propel squid

Devil in the dark
The deep-sea vampire squid spends its life in constant darkness, but its body produces light – a phenomenon called bioluminescence. The squid flashes its light to lure prey and attract mates. If this brings unwanted attention, it folds its webbed tentacles over the mantle, and shuts out the light.

Webbed tentacle

Going flat
Flatfish, such as this flounder, go through an amazing change. A young flounder swims upright like other fish, but as it grows, its skull twists so that the right eye moves to the left side of the head. This way both eyes are on the same side of the head, and it can look for prey while lying camouflaged on the sea bed.

Freshwater living

Inland water habitats can be as challenging to life as the oceans. Many aquatic animals rely on unpredictable little streams and ponds, which may freeze in winter and dry out in summer. Slow-flowing water loses oxygen and fish cannot use their gills effectively, while fast-flowing streams are a difficult environment to live in. In addition, animal body tissues, which are full of salts, pull water in from fresh water, so freshwater animals must constantly produce watery urine to flush it out.

White plumage turned pink by diet

Thick skin resists chemicals in water

Mineral rich
Not every inland body of water is fresh. Flamingos live in desert lakes filled with salts and other chemicals. They survive by feeding on tough brine shrimps, which live on a diet of bacteria (small single-celled organisms).

Beak has plates that sift food from water

Bony scute protects body

Lurking in the shallows
This spectacled caiman, like other crocodilians, is superbly suited to hunting in shallow waters. It lies hidden under the water with only the eyes and nostrils above the surface, ready to surge up the bank to drag prey into the water. A crocodile's bite is 10 times stronger than that of a shark, and once its victim is in the water, death is almost certain. The caiman also eats large quantities of fish.

On their own
Freshwater lakes are isolated habitats with unique wildlife, in much the same way as remote islands far out at sea. Lake Baikal, the world's largest lake, in eastern Russia, is home to the only freshwater species of seal, known as the nerpa. The ancestors of the nerpa swam upriver from the sea about 80,000 years ago., but their route back to the ocean has since disappeared.

Survivors

Tardigrades, or water bears, are microscopic animals that live in all types of water – from hot springs to muddy puddles – and graze on bacteria. They are the toughest creatures alive. When the water dries out or becomes too salty, a tardigrade hauls up its eight legs and becomes dormant. Scientists have found that tardigrades can even survive in space.

Spider falls into water after being hit by water

Tree ponds

Freshwater habitats can be found in some unusual places. The leaves of succulent jungle plants called bromeliads form a cup that collects rainwater. These little ponds, high up in the trees, are used by many poison dart frogs to raise their young. If the baby outgrows its pool, the mother carries it to a larger one.

Stream of droplets

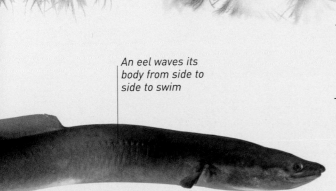

An eel waves its body from side to side to swim

Water cannon

The archerfish uses water as a weapon. It pokes its lips above the surface, and fires a jet of water out of its mouth with a quick squeeze of its gill covers. The jet can travel up to 3 m (10 ft) into the air, knocking its prey from overhanging leaves into the water. The archerfish mostly hits its target at the first attempt, because its eyes and brain can adjust to the bending of light that happens when light moves from air to water.

A watery road

Most aquatic (water-living) animals are adapted to one habitat, but the common eel has specialized kidneys that enable it to live in both salty and fresh water. This snake-shaped fish starts life in the Sargasso Sea. Baby eels, or elvers, head across the Atlantic Ocean to river mouths in Europe, where fresh water mixes with salty sea water. Some stay there, but most elvers head inland, even slithering over land to reach a suitable freshwater habitat. Once mature, the adult eels go back to sea to breed.

Hawker naiad spears a stickleback fish

Wet nursery

Very few insect species live in marine habitats, but many, such as the hawker dragonfly, start life in fresh water. This young dragonfly – known as a naiad – breathes with gills and uses a sharp mouthpart to spear prey with lightning speed. After several months of hunting in shallow pools, the naiad climbs up the stalk of a water plant and transforms into an adult.

Cold and ice

The coldest habitats on Earth are near the Poles, where summers are too short to provide much warmth, and high up on mountains, where the air is too thin to retain heat. Most of the animals that live in cold places are warm-blooded, though a few cold-blooded species have evolved adaptations that enable them to survive in cold conditions. Some insects can freeze in winter, but still be alive and well when they thaw out in spring.

Big is best
The bodies of large animals lose heat slowly in cold conditions, which is why animals in cold regions tend to be larger than those in warmer ones. The world's largest deer, the moose, lives in the cold north, as does the musk ox, the largest goat, and the gyrfalcon, the biggest falcon. Polar animals also tend to have shorter legs, ears, and tails, which also helps reduce heat loss.

Found in plenty
The polar oceans are so cold that the surface of the water freezes over at times. The conditions under the water are less severe, however, and the polar seas thrive with life. Krill – tiny relatives of shrimps – swarm in their millions, providing an important food source for marine life.

Antarctic krill

Life in the Arctic
Earth's polar regions experience extreme seasonal changes. Most polar bears are active throughout the year, but pregnant females enter a hibernation-like state and sleep through the winter. Bear cubs are born at this time, growing strong on their mother's milk while she sleeps. Mother and cubs are ready to hunt as soon as summer arrives.

Pale fur camouflages bear among the ice

Wide feet do not sink into snow and help make bears strong swimmers

Wing is larger than those of other geese

High fliers

Bar-headed geese are some of the highest flying birds. They cross over the Himalayas while migrating from the wetlands in India to the Tibetan plateau. The temperature can drop to -30 °C (-22 °F), and the air is so thin that the geese breathe hundreds of times in a minute to get enough oxygen.

Happy feet

Body heat can cause problems in freezing conditions. Warm skin melts ice, but the ice freezes again almost instantly, bonding to the skin in the same way that a tongue sticks to an ice lolly. Amazingly, emperor penguins can survive at -60 °C (-76 °F), the coldest conditions experienced by any animal. Warm blood pumping into the feet loses heat to cold blood flowing back to the heart, so the feet stay cold and never get warm enough to melt the ice.

Chick sits on father's feet to stay off cold ice

Best foot forward

This mountain goat lives on steep cliffs in British Columbia, Canada, where only the most sure-footed animals can survive. A mountain goat's hoof has two parts, which spread apart and grab the rough ground like a pincer. The sharp rim of the hoof digs into the ice, helping to grip the surface, while the base is covered in a spongy pad that prevents the animal from slipping.

Iceberg ahead

A beluga whale lives along the edge of the Arctic sea ice. Its white skin disguises it among the floating icebergs and helps it hide from orcas and polar bears. The beluga is hairless and keeps warm thanks to a 10-cm- (4-in-) thick layer of fatty blubber under its skin. It is nicknamed the sea canary because it communicates using whistles and chirps.

Small ear reduces heat loss

In the desert

About one-fifth of Earth's land is very dry and receives less than 250 mm (10 in) of rain in a year – less than a bucketful. These regions are deserts, and range from the Sahara and other searing hot, tropical deserts to cold deserts, such as the Gobi in central Asia. Desert animals must cope with temperatures that plummet at night, and go for long periods without food or anything to drink.

Wedge-shaped snout slices through sand

Leg held against body as lizard slithers like a snake

Swimming in the sand
A sandfish is actually a specialized skink – a type of lizard. Its strong, cylindrical body and short legs help it slither through loose sand. The creature hunts on the sand, detecting tiny vibrations made by insects.

Thick fur keeps camel warm in cold, high desert

Bactrian camel has two humps

Fat reserves
Water drains through sandy desert soil quickly, so there are few places where plants can grow. Desert browsers, such as this Bactrian camel of central Asia, can go without water for 10 days and survive on the toughest desert shrubs. The camel carries a supply of food in its humps, in the form of oily fats.

Wing cases are fused shut, stopping body from drying out

Drinking the fog
The huge sand dunes of Africa's Namib Desert rise up on the coast of the Atlantic Ocean. While rainfall is rare, dense banks of fog often roll in from the sea. Fog-basking beetles sit at the top of the dunes and literally drink the mist. Each beetle does a handstand, and tiny droplets condense on its body, running down grooves that lead to its mouth.

Following the rain

The Arabian oryx, a type of antelope, goes for weeks without drinking, getting all the water it needs from the plants it feeds on. It can smell rain from kilometres away, and travels towards fresh plants that grow after rainfall. When not on the move, an oryx digs a cool pit in the sand and rests in the shade.

Surviving the heat

Frogs need to stay moist in the desert heat. The Australian water-holding frog keeps damp by digging deep into the ground and cocooning itself in a bag of mucus. The cocoon hardens and forms a water-tight barrier that locks in water around the frog's body. The amphibian stays underground until it rains again.

Keeping cool

Large mammals can get very hot under the Sun. Their body temperature can rise above 41 °C (105.8 °F) to levels that would damage the brain of many mammals. A gazelle remains quite unaffected – its cooling system chills the blood entering its brain. This allows the gazelle to keep on running when being chased by a predator, while its pursuer must stop to avoid overheating.

A gazelle's brain-cooling system

Some warm blood reaches brain directly

Cooled blood travels to rest of body

Warm blood to brain passes through cool sinus

Sinus (chamber) filled with cooled blood

Blood in network of thin vessels is cooled by air

Water in fog condenses on beetle's cold body

Sun spiders

Deserts are home to sun spiders, some of the fiercest predators in the animal kingdom. At about 15 cm (6 in) long, its large pincerlike mouthparts make up one-quarter of its body. It uses its vast pincers to slice beetles and other insects. A sun spider will even tackle desert mice.

Sun spider with prey

Fill the tank

Sandgrouse live in the dry parts of Europe, Africa, and Asia. They are seed eaters, and flock to deserts when flowering plants are in seed. The adult birds fly great distances to find watering holes. They then soak their belly feathers in water to airlift drinks to their chicks.

Open grassland

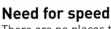

Pronghorn, a North American, hoofed grassland, mammal

Grasslands grow in areas that are too dry for forests to flourish, but not dry enough for deserts to form. There is enough rain for fast-growing grasses to grow, which provide enough food for the animals that live there. There are no specific food sources to defend, so plant-eating animals, such as bulky bulls, compete over other things, such as the chance to mate.

Need for speed

There are no places to hide on grasslands, so when danger appears, hoofed animals, such as antelopes and pronghorns, run fast. The pronghorn is capable of reaching speeds of up to 100 kph (60 mph). Hoofed animals stand on their tiptoes. Their feet are long, and this helps them to lengthen their legs and increase their stride.

Snake in the grass

This reptile is not a snake, but a lizard that slithers along without legs. It lives in European and Asian grasslands, where it hunts slugs. It is named the glass lizard because it appears to break in two, like a piece of brittle glasses when picked up by the tail.

Termites

The most important grazers (grass eaters) in some grasslands are tiny insects – termites. Like an ant's nest, a termite colony has a queen, but unlike an ant's nest, it also has a king. Millions of termites live in tall mounds, made of mud reinforced with dried grass. A natural cooling system reduces the heat produced by the termites.

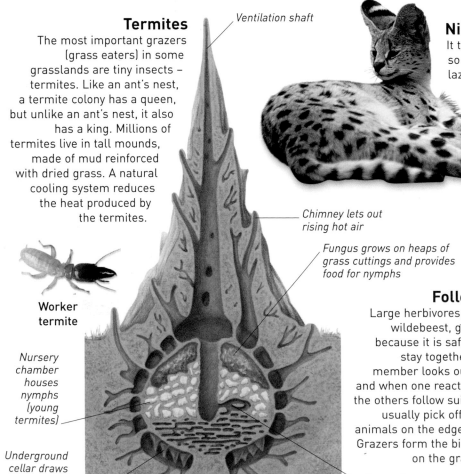

Ventilation shaft

Chimney lets out rising hot air

Fungus grows on heaps of grass cuttings and provides food for nymphs

Worker termite

Nursery chamber houses nymphs (young termites)

Underground cellar draws in cool air from outside mound

Queen lives in a royal chamber

Night hunter

It too easy to be spotted by prey during daylight, so many grassland predators spend their days lazing in the shade, waiting until dark. The serval, an African cat about twice the size of a house cat, uses its large ears to listen for rodents in the grass.

Follow the herd

Large herbivores, such as these wildebeest, gather in herds because it is safer for them to stay together. Every herd member looks out for danger, and when one reacts to a threat, the others follow suit. Predators usually pick off the weaker animals on the edges of a herd. Grazers form the biggest herds on the grassy plains.

Silent stalker

Unlike other birds of prey that swoop over grasslands, the secretary bird hunts on foot. Stalking slowly through short grass on its stiltlike legs, this gangle bird watches the ground intently, and when a lizard, locust, or other small animal comes out from a hiding place, it traps it with its foot. It kills its victim with a rip from its hooked beak.

Nesting underground

Temperate (cool) grasslands, such as the American prairies, have almost no trees at all. The American burrowing owl, therefore, nests underground. It usually does not dig the den, but sets up home in a hole vacated by another burrowing animal, such as a prairie dog. The burrow provides the owl with a shelter from predators.

Among the trees

More animals are found in forests than in any other habitat on Earth. Forests range from hot, damp jungles to cold conifer woodlands in the far north. A single tropical rainforest tree can house more than a thousand species. In all cases, the tall trees provide hundreds of different habitats. As a result, forests are home to both noisy howler monkeys and quiet sloths.

Cuvier's toucan

Fruits and nuts

This toucan is a frugivore (fruit eater). Frugivores live only in tropical forests in which warm temperatures allow year-round fruiting. The bird's colourful bill is long enough to reach fruits dangling from flimsy branches, and its jagged edge is strong enough to crack open nuts.

Hidden away

The jaguar is the biggest jungle cat in America. In the dappled light of the forest, the cat's distinctive pattern of blotchy rosettes (roselike markings) makes for perfect camouflage. This helps the predator hide in the foliage and sneak up on deer and other prey.

Target in sight

In the trees, a vine snake has only one chance to catch its prey before it has gone. The snake has a groove that runs from each eye to the tip of its snout that works like a gun sight. It lines up the grooves to zero in on mice and small birds.

Groove helps target prey

Foraging on the floor

Most of the time, this giant millipede remains hidden away among leaf litter – the thick layer of dead leaves that covers the floor of a forest. It grazes on dead plant material on the forest floor, which is also the hunting ground for predatory centipedes and blind snakes.

Up the tree

Moisture-loving frogs can easily survive high up in the branches of rainforests. Tree frogs crawl along leaves, using cup-shaped suckers on their toes to grip the flat surfaces. This red-eyed tree frog keeps its eyes shut tight when hiding. If threatened by a predator, the frog stares squarely at it and flashes its startling blue and yellow body colours.

Vertical pupil tracks moving insects

Bright orange foot startles predators

Tail can support weight of monkey's body

Loose skin on sole of foot helps grip

Getting noticed

Sometimes animals need to get noticed to attract mates. When resting with its wings folded, the blue morpho butterfly may look drab among the leaves. However, when it flies, the top of the wings are revealed, showing off a shimmering blue colour.

Hanging out

When living so high up, just one foot out of place could be fatal. The New World monkeys of South America get a helping hand from their prehensile tail, which can wrap around a branch. The tail has a hairless pad at the tip that also aids grip. This woolly monkey can hang from its tail alone.

Emergent tree 38 m (125 ft)

Canopy 28 m (92 ft)

Understorey 17 m (56 ft)

Undergrowth 5 m (16 ft)

Forest floor

The right fit

Jungle mammals tend to be smaller than those living in open habitats, such as grasslands. Being smaller helps this African forest elephant when pushing through thick foliage. Jungle birds, on the other hand, appear to have longer bills, or beaks, than their relatives living in cooler places. The birds might use a large beak as a radiator to give out heat, so their bodies do not overheat as they fly through the steamy forest.

Many levels

Tropical rainforests have layers that function as habitats for different groups of animals. At the top are occasional giant trees called emergents. They and the canopy trees are out in the sunshine, but they block out the light, making the forest floor a gloomy place. The canopy forms a continuous layer that is home to most rainforest animals.

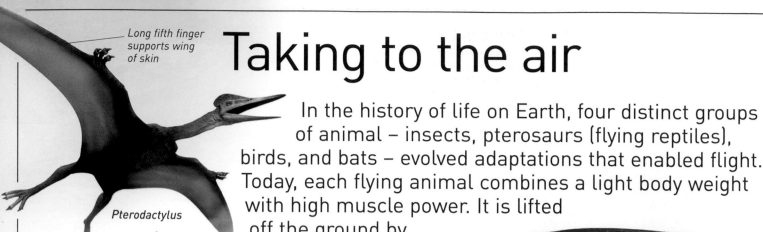

Long fifth finger supports wing of skin

Pterodactylus

Taking to the air

In the history of life on Earth, four distinct groups of animal – insects, pterosaurs (flying reptiles), birds, and bats – evolved adaptations that enabled flight. Today, each flying animal combines a light body weight with high muscle power. It is lifted off the ground by wings. As the wings cut through the air, they create a lift force that opposes gravity, and raises or holds the animal in the air.

Flying reptiles

The first flying vertebrates were the pterosaurs. These reptiles were closely related to dinosaurs and became extinct at the same time, around 65 million years ago. One of the first fossil pterosaurs discovered was *Pterodactylus*, meaning "wing finger" – its wing was mostly skin stretched behind a single long finger bone.

Primary flight feather

Small claw on thumb is used for gripping when bat is at rest

Handy wings

Bats, which appeared around 50 million years ago, were the last group of animals to take to the air. They are the only mammals that can fly. A bat's skin wing stretches between its finger bones. Although bats can see, many rely mostly on a system called echolocation to find their way. Bats emit high-pitched chirps that echo from objects around them. Based on the echoes, they then work out the distances to the objects, forming a sound picture of their surroundings.

Wing membrane stretches between thin finger bones

Secondary flight feather

Wing is a thin membrane running between stiff veins

Wing twists as it moves up, cutting through the air, but flattens again as it flaps down, pushing against the air

Wing is powered by muscles at its base

Four wings first

Insects were the first animals to fly. No other invertebrate group has taken to the air since. It is believed that the first flying insects, which appeared around 350 million years ago, had four wings and looked like today's dragonflies. Insect wings are not modified legs, like those of birds and bats, and may have evolved from gills of aquatic larvae.

Back wing moves in opposite direction to front wings in slow flight, to reduce speed while continuing to provide the lifting force for flight

Staying put

Hummingbirds use their long feathery tongues to lap nectar from delicate flowers while hovering in mid-air. The birds beat their wings up to 20 times a second to hover, making the wings look like a blur. To beat this fast, hummingbirds have very flexible triangular wings, but such wings are not well suited for flying long distances.

Masters of the air

Birds are the most varied and widespread flying animals. Different birds have different wing shapes that enable many kinds of flying style. For example, this heron has broad wings that allow slow gliding, while a swift's pointed wings let it swoop at high speed. A bird's bones are thin, hollow, and lightweight – a third of its body weight is in the strong flight muscles in its plump breast.

Toe is very long and supports large "parachute" area

Falling not flying

Wallace's flying frog lives high in the trees of Southeast Asia's jungles. It leaps into the air to escape predators and to reach mates in pools on the forest floor. The frog's large webbed feet break its fall like a parachute, but this is not the same as flying.

Neck vertebra (neck bone)

Humerus (upper arm bone)

Pollex (thumb bone)

Finger bone

Radius (a lower arm bone)

Metacarpal (fused hand bone)

Backbone

Skeleton of grey heron

Hip bone

Ulna (a lower arm bone)

Tail feather

Tibia (shin bone)

Coloured X-ray of flying fish

Ankle

Fins in a flap

The wings of a flying fish are stiffened fins that catch updrafts of air pushed up by waves rolling across the surface of the ocean. The fish leaps into the air to escape attacks from predators, such as tuna. A flying fish surges along the surface, swishing its tail dozens of times a second, until it glides into the air, typically up to a distance of around 50 m (160 ft).

Toe bone

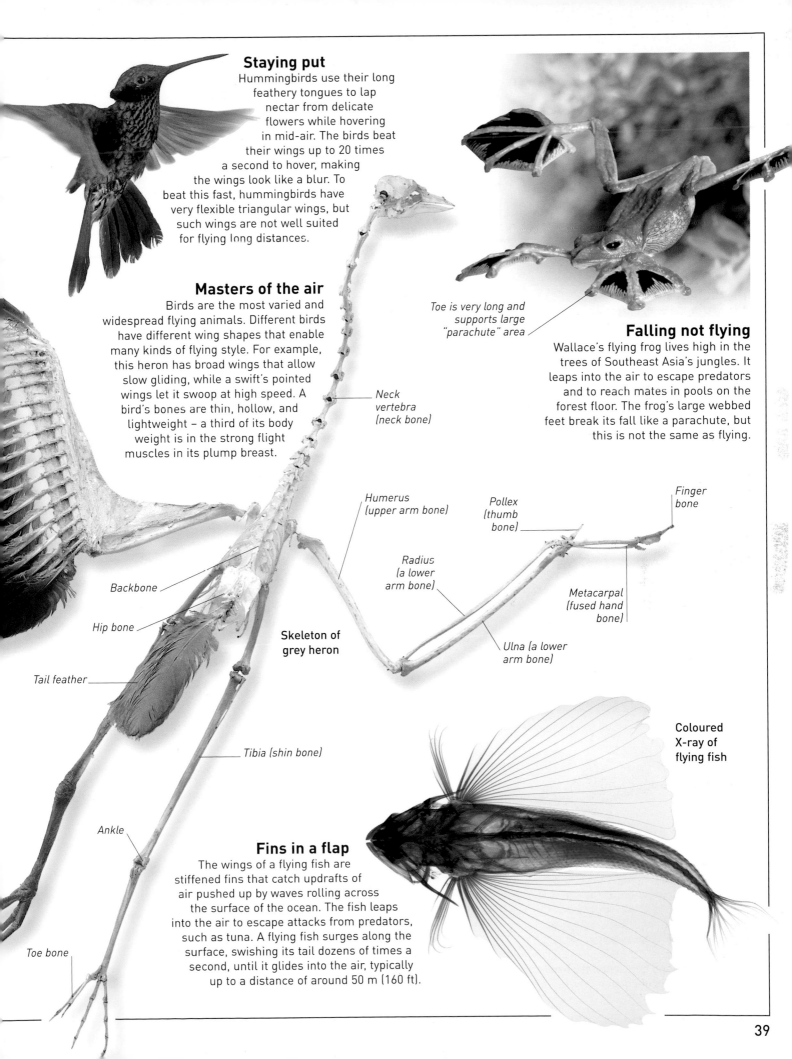

Animal homes

Some animals are always on the move, searching for food and mates. Others live in one area, defending their territory from other members of their species. Still others set up temporary homes to hibernate or raise their young. A bird's nest is perhaps the best known example of an animal's home, but even large mammals, such as gorillas, build nests.

Stitched homes

The masked weaver bird knits grass together to build a woven ball hanging from a tree. Only the male weavers create nests, and different males often build them in the same tree. When the nests are ready, female weavers inspect them. If a female likes a nest, she pairs with its builder as she considers him a good mate with which to raise chicks.

House of leaves

Weaver ants live in trees and they make their nests out of the material available. Teams of worker ants haul the edges of leaves together, while other adults bind the leaves together with a sticky silk, produced by larvae. Adults hold larvae like tubes of glue to form a boxlike, green nest.

Silk produced by ant larvae glues together edges of leaves

1 Best location

The male first chooses a small branch to hang the nest from. He prefers to locate it near the tops of trees, out of reach of climbing predators, such as snakes, and often near a source of water.

Diving bell

The web made by a water spider is not a sticky fly trap. Instead, it holds the spider's air supply during hunting dives. The spider retreats to its bubble home to digest food. Its web works like a gill, releasing waste carbon dioxide and taking in oxygen from the water. Every so often, the spider refills the web with fresh air at the surface.

Case made from plant stems and pebbles

Front end enlarges as larva grows inside

A bits-and-pieces home

Caddisfly larvae live in freshwater streams. Some species weave a silk tube to live in, which acts as a net to catch specks of food. Other caddisflies use their silk to glue bits of the riverbed into an armoured case. This case is open at both ends and the insect draws in water, providing the animal with food and oxygen.

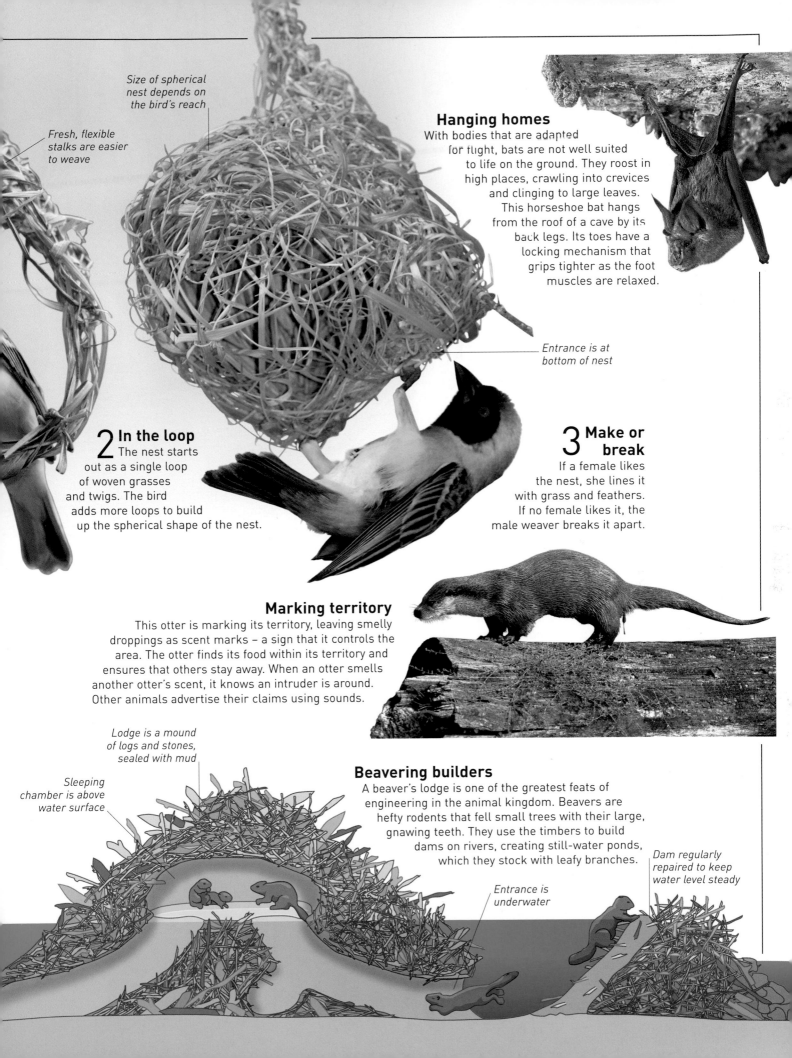

Fresh, flexible stalks are easier to weave

Size of spherical nest depends on the bird's reach

Hanging homes

With bodies that are adapted for flight, bats are not well suited to life on the ground. They roost in high places, crawling into crevices and clinging to large leaves. This horseshoe bat hangs from the roof of a cave by its back legs. Its toes have a locking mechanism that grips tighter as the foot muscles are relaxed.

Entrance is at bottom of nest

2 In the loop

The nest starts out as a single loop of woven grasses and twigs. The bird adds more loops to build up the spherical shape of the nest.

3 Make or break

If a female likes the nest, she lines it with grass and feathers. If no female likes it, the male weaver breaks it apart.

Marking territory

This otter is marking its territory, leaving smelly droppings as scent marks – a sign that it controls the area. The otter finds its food within its territory and ensures that others stay away. When an otter smells another otter's scent, it knows an intruder is around. Other animals advertise their claims using sounds.

Lodge is a mound of logs and stones, sealed with mud

Sleeping chamber is above water surface

Beavering builders

A beaver's lodge is one of the greatest feats of engineering in the animal kingdom. Beavers are hefty rodents that fell small trees with their large, gnawing teeth. They use the timbers to build dams on rivers, creating still-water ponds, which they stock with leafy branches.

Dam regularly repaired to keep water level steady

Entrance is underwater

Migrations

A migration is a journey that an animal undertakes, often along a set route. It is neither an aimless search for food nor simply patrolling territory. A migration has start and end points, and the animal always makes a return journey, or its descendants do. Animals migrate in response to changes in the seasons, which make it hard for them to survive. The sight of thousands of creatures on the move is one of nature's great spectacles.

Birds take turns to lead flock

Birthing site

Humpback whales spend the summer in the rich feeding grounds of polar seas. However, this water is too cold for newborn calves. They are born without the thick blubber that keeps the adults warm. Therefore, in winter, these whales migrate to warmer seas near the equator to give birth. The calves then return with their mothers.

Head contains a mineral called magnetite, possibly helping the bird track Earth's magnetic field

Following the stream

The life cycle of each of these colourful sockeye salmon is one long migration. The fish start out in the headwaters of a river. As they grow, they head downstream, finally reaching the sea, where they mature over several years. The adult salmon travel all the way upriver to their birthplace to spawn, after which they die.

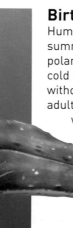

Antennae rubbing makes rasping noises that frighten attackers

Walking the ocean

These spiny lobsters march in line across the sandy sea bed of the Caribbean during their autumn migration to warmer waters. The lobsters also head for deeper waters, perhaps to escape the storms that disrupt their shallow summer territory.

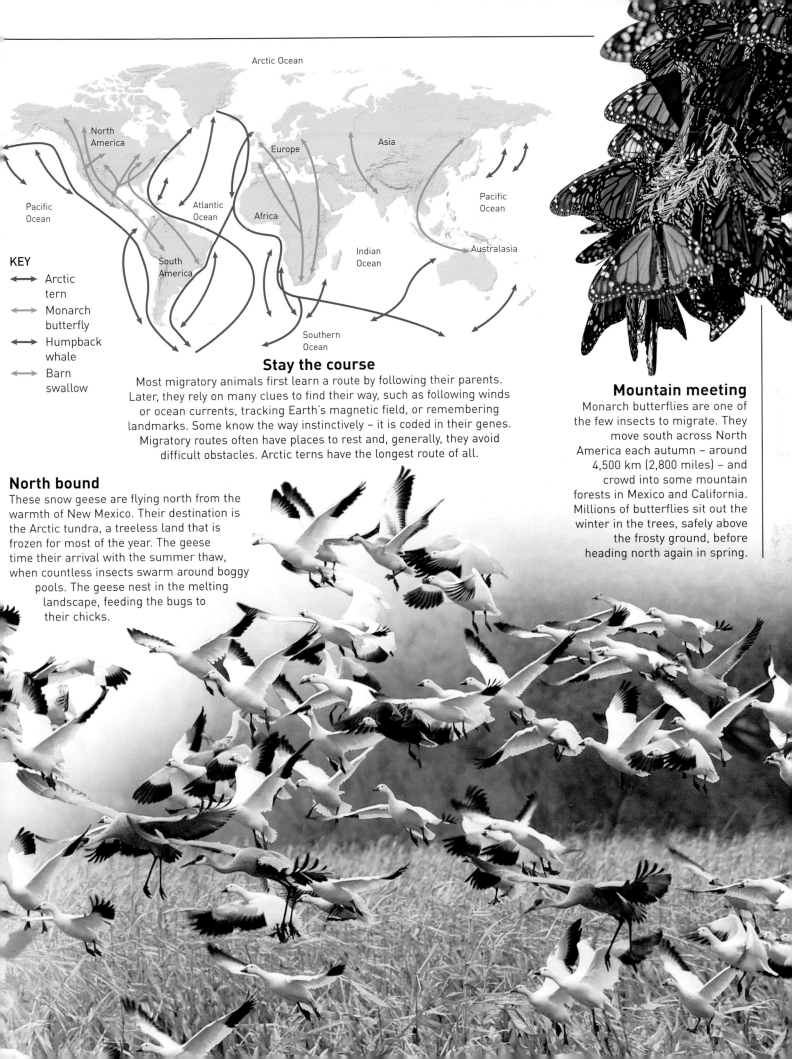

KEY

← → Arctic tern
← → Monarch butterfly
← → Humpback whale
← → Barn swallow

Stay the course

Most migratory animals first learn a route by following their parents. Later, they rely on many clues to find their way, such as following winds or ocean currents, tracking Earth's magnetic field, or remembering landmarks. Some know the way instinctively – it is coded in their genes. Migratory routes often have places to rest and, generally, they avoid difficult obstacles. Arctic terns have the longest route of all.

North bound

These snow geese are flying north from the warmth of New Mexico. Their destination is the Arctic tundra, a treeless land that is frozen for most of the year. The geese time their arrival with the summer thaw, when countless insects swarm around boggy pools. The geese nest in the melting landscape, feeding the bugs to their chicks.

Mountain meeting

Monarch butterflies are one of the few insects to migrate. They move south across North America each autumn – around 4,500 km (2,800 miles) – and crowd into some mountain forests in Mexico and California. Millions of butterflies sit out the winter in the trees, safely above the frosty ground, before heading north again in spring.

Staying alive

In the wild, animals face a constant struggle for survival. Predators must kill prey for food, while prey must always be ready to fend off a predator's attack. Both predator and prey are in a race to stay a step ahead of each other, each animal adapting constantly in the presence of an evolving foe. When a mouse evolves resistance to a snake's venom, the snake evolves in ways that make it more toxic – both predator and prey evolve constantly, but neither gains an advantage.

Hidden trickster

The Peringuey's adder lives in the deserts of southwest Africa. This snake is not easy to spot – its rough scales match the sand and it lies waiting to ambush prey, such as this gecko. The snake lures the lizard within biting distance by wiggling the dark tip of its tail. The adder's venom kills its prey in seconds.

Dry outer strand is held by spider

Traps of silk

The ogre-faced spider eats insects on the ground. These insects are sensitive to vibrations and are ready to scuttle for safety at the slightest scare. But this long-legged spider avoids detection by hanging motionless just above the ground, flexing a sticky net in its four front legs. It waits for an insect to walk to under the net, and then moves with lightning speed to snare it.

One whale dives to make bubble net

Fish "baitball" driven to surface

Waiting whale

Whale blowing bubbles

Waiting whale's calls scare fish into a tight shoal

Spiral path followed by whale

Bubbles rise to the surface

Bubble nets

For humpback whales, eating a few fish at a time takes far too long to fill their stomachs. So they band together to herd fish into tight shoals that are perfect for eating in gulps. The whales swim in a spiral, blowing a curtain of bubbles, and making the fish crowd together at the surface. Then, they surge up from below with their mouths gaping open.

Eye spot looks like a large animal's eyes

Mimics

This owl butterfly would make an easy meal for a rainforest tree frog. But the hungry frog stays away from it because when the butterfly opens its wings, two dark spots suddenly appear. This fools the frog into believing that it is looking into the eyes of a dangerous owl.

Diving down
A kingfisher has evolved eyes that allow it to spot fish before entering the water. Water bends light, so the bird has to adjust its eyes when targeting underwater prey. Each of the bird's eyes has two focus points – one for use out of the water and the other for after it dives in. The eyes of most animals have just one. The cells in a kingfisher's eyes also contain a pigmented oil that probably filters out the glare from water.

Spraying acid
In any colony, only the queen ant produces young, so it is common for worker ants to sacrifice themselves to protect her. To ward off predators, wood ants employ chemical weapons. They squirt formic acid from their abdomens – the same chemical that causes the burning pain of a bee sting.

Transparent eyelid slides across eye to protect it

Tail regrows slowly

Two lives
The tree skink has a quick-release bone at the base of its tail, which snaps off. If grabbed by the tail, the lizard can escape. The predator is left with a wriggling detached tail. The skink regenerates a new tail, but this one does not detach in the next attack.

Living together

Animals frequently rely on another animal species for their survival. Such a link is called symbiosis, which means "together living" in Ancient Greek. There are three kinds of symbiosis. In parasitism, only one species benefits from the relationship, while the other – known as the host – is weakened by it. Mutualism is a relationship in which both species benefit, while in commensalism one animal benefits, while the other is completely unaffected.

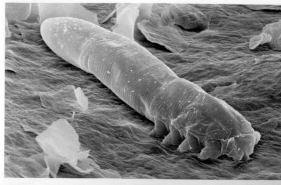

Tiny passenger
About 50 per cent of people live in symbiosis with this microscopic eyelash mite. This mite sets up home in the follicle (a small sac or cavity from which a hair grows) of the human eyelash, eating oily flakes of skin.

Plaintive cuckoo chick

Cuckoo in the nest
This chick is being fed by a male sunbird, but this bird is not the chick's father. The chick is a cuckoo, and its mother laid the egg in the sunbird's nest. The cuckoo is a brood parasite – an animal that tricks another into raising its young. A cuckoo's egg looks a lot like a sunbird egg, so the sunbird fails to spot the interloper. Once the chick hatches, it ejects any sunbird chicks or unhatched sunbird eggs.

Wingless aphid sucks sap constantly

Aphid farms
Aphids are insects that drink plant sap. With a purely liquid diet, the little aphids produce a lot of sugary urine, known as honeydew. Some ants will stand guard over a herd of aphids, keeping away predators. The ants "milk" the aphids, stroking them to make them produce sweet droplets of honeydew. This relationship is an example of mutualism.

Male mariqua sunbird

Pecking to order

The oxpecker is a relative of the starling. It lives among the herds of grazing mammals, such as this zebra, that roam across the grasslands of Africa. It slides its flat beak between the hairs of the host to pluck ticks and lice from its host's skin. The zebra gets a cleaning service, while the bird is rewarded with tasty, blood-sucking parasites. The oxpecker may also act as a parasite, feeding on blood from open wounds.

Big eye of watchman goby its name

Teaming up

The watchman goby and the pistol shrimp team up on the sandy sea bed. The shrimp digs a burrow, while the fish acts as the short-sighted shrimp's lookout. If danger approaches, the goby flicks the shrimp with its tail, and the duo dash inside.

Shrimp keeps the burrow clean

Ridged sucker is formed from a flattened dorsal fin

Remora

Hyena stands over its food in a defensive posture

Thieving carnivores

Spotted hyenas are scavengers that feast on the carcasses of animals. Often a hyena gang will chase a hunter, such as a big cat, away from its kill. This behaviour is called kleptoparasitism. But the hyena's meal is not safe either – other thieves may try to snatch a bite.

Going with the flow

Commensalism is rare compared to the other forms of symbiosis. The remora sticks itself to large sharks, rays, and whales, using a sucker on the top of its head. The fish eats its host's droppings or the leftovers from the host's meals. The larger animal neither gains nor benefits.

Black-backed jackal – another kleptoparasite – is wary of the hyena

Living in groups

Humans are not the only animals that live in societies. There are advantages and disadvantages to being a social animal. Group members have to share many things, such as food. Adult males may also have to compete for the same females in the group. Despite these problems, the members of a group stick together. In all cases, animal societies function as a delicate balance where the gains outweigh the losses.

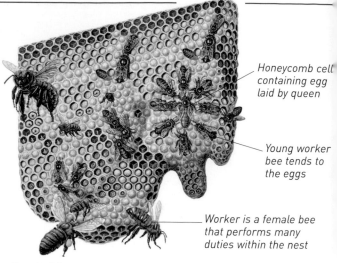

Honeycomb cell containing egg laid by queen

Young worker bee tends to the eggs

Worker is a female bee that performs many duties within the nest

Social bees
Honeybees have an advanced level of social organization that is also seen in ants, termites, some wasps, and even rodents. A single female – the queen bee – produces the offspring. The rest of the society is made up of her daughters, who work to raise their younger sisters – and occasionally brothers, or drones, who fly off to mate with young queens. The worker bees never produce young of their own. They collect nectar to make honey to feed the colony.

Pairing up
The smallest animal group is a breeding pair. In lovebirds – a small species of parrot – the male and a female pair up for life. Even if the two birds spend long periods apart, they meet up and raise chicks together when the breeding season comes. This single-mate system is called monogamy. These pairs work together to protect their young and maximize their chances of survival.

Fisher's lovebirds

Superpods at sea
Dolphins and whales live in family groups called pods, which typically contain about 15 animals. They are made up of females, their calves, and a tight-knit gang of males. When several pods converge at one place to feed, a superpod forms.

Rank and file

Hamadryas baboons of East Africa and Arabia live in a highly ordered society. In a troop of around 400 monkeys, every monkey has a rank. Big adult males rule over a harem of females, and several harems band together as a clan – one of many per troop. Males frequently fight over females – young males are always ready to take over from an older, weakening male – but if a monkey steps out of line, it is punished with a bite.

Dominant male has tufts of gray fur

Baby travels with its mother

Young male is not allowed to mate

Female may be stolen by another harem

Hunting in a team

The wolf is one of the few animals that can kill prey that is bigger than it is. It does this by working in a team, or pack. Wolves can follow prey for hours on end without getting tired, so the pack chases prey, such as an injured deer, taking turns to bite their victim until it crashes to the ground.

Wolves howl to warn other packs to stay away

Population explosion

Locust swarms are some of the largest animal groupings, containing billions of insects. These large grasshoppers normally live on their own, but crowd together in search of food. Increased levels of body contact cause the insects to create a different kind of young. When these transform into long-winged adults, they fly off as a swarm.

One of the crowd

Seabirds, such as these gannets, nest together in huge colonies, called rookeries. The cliffs are so inaccessible that egg eaters, such as rats, cannot reach them. The parents take turns to dive for food out at sea, bringing some back for the chicks. They tap beaks on returning to identify each other.

Livestock

Thousands of years ago, humans began to domesticate and rear useful animals, using them for their muscle power, products, and body parts. The first livestock (farm animals) were sheep and goats, which were probably domesticated around 8,000 years ago. Gradually, the list of livestock grew to include cattle, pigs, and chickens. Farmers bred animals so that their offspring would have the most useful traits, and, as a result, livestock is tame.

Horn is shaped partly by the human owner

Owner's pride
The word cattle comes from the Old French word "chatel", meaning property. In several societies, cattle are symbols of wealth and status. These zebus (humped cattle), for instance, belong to the Dinka people of Southern Sudan. A single cow provides manure (used as fertilizer and fuel), milk, and even blood to drink. When a zebu dies, its skin is made into leather.

Aurochs – the ancestor of modern cattle

Scottish Aberdeen Angus is bred for good quality meat

Then and now
The domestic cow is a descendant of a grazer called the aurochs. Once spread across Europe and Asia, aurochs became extinct in 1627. Zebus (main picture) are descended from Indian aurochs, while beef cattle are related to European aurochs.

A living ancestor
Every domestic animal is a descendant of a wild ancestor. Many of these wild animals are extinct or have become very rare. However, red jungle fowl – believed to be the wild form of the chicken – are still widespread in Southeast Asia. Males display the same vibrant features of a farmyard cockerel.

Red jungle fowl cockerel

Wild inside
Despite centuries of captive breeding to shape domestic animals into tame and productive creatures, some still exhibit certain wild characteristics. For example, sheep dash uphill when frightened – just as their ancestor, the small and sturdy mouflon, would do when they needed to escape attackers in the rocky mountains of western Asia.

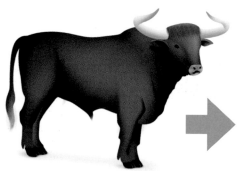

Woolly jumper

For millennia, humans have used the fur of other mammals to stay warm in cold climates. Woolly hairs can be spun into strands or yarn, and used to weave warm clothing. Wool comes from sheep, alpacas, camels, and goats. Perhaps the softest wool comes from fluffy angora rabbits.

Bug to dye for

In the 16th century, red dyes in Europe were too expensive for all but the wealthiest families. Spanish settlers in South America were, therefore, intrigued by how the local people dyed their clothes deep red. Cochineal bugs, which live on cacti, produce a chemical that is used to make the dye.

Silk Route

The Silk Route – an ancient trade route that ran from China in the East to the Mediterranean in the West – was named after silk, the most lucrative product to be traded along it. In the West, the secret of the production of fine silk strands was unknown, but they are produced by silkworms – moth caterpillars that live on mulberry tree leaves. These silkworms are kept at a breeding base in Matou town, China.

Animal workers

The first working animals may have acted as guards. These half-tamed wolves may have lived alongside humans about 15,000 years ago. These animals barked to warn humans of approaching danger. Before the invention of engines, many machines, such as wheeled carts and water pumps, were powered by animals. Today, humans use many animals for their natural abilities.

To the rescue
This search dog uses its sense of smell to find people buried in snow. A dog's smell senses are far superior to a human's, because the odour-detecting part of its brain is 40 times bigger than the same section in a human brain. There are also about 195 million more smell receptors in a dog's wet nose.

Tracking device attached to flipper

Animal soldiers
This bottlenose dolphin works for the US Navy. The brain of a dolphin is larger than that of a human, but not as complex. Nevertheless, the dolphin is highly intelligent, and can be trained to recognize enemy mines suspended in the water. Other navy dolphins are trained to search for injured human divers.

Hard worker
A mule's father (sire) is a donkey, but its mother (dam) is a horse. They cannot produce young of their own – they are born to work as beasts of burden. Mules have the best features of their parents. They are big and strong like a horse, but calm and sure-footed like a donkey.

Catching fish

The cormorant is an expert fish catcher, and Chinese fishermen have been using its skills for more than a thousand years. A loose snare around a cormorant's neck will allow it to swallow small fish, while bigger ones get stuck. When a bird returns to the boat, its owner gently eases the fish from the bird's throat.

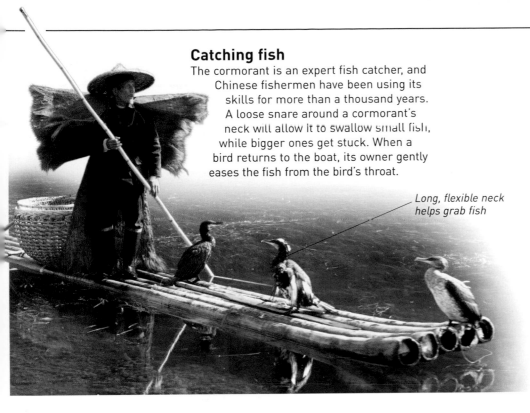

Long, flexible neck helps grab fish

China statuette of Lipizzaner dancing horse

Dancing horses

Lipizzaner horses come from Slovenia. These horses have descended from Spanish and North African varieties, and were bred to be strong and agile. While adult Lipizzaners are white, foals are born much darker. Some stallions are trained to dance.

Easy to study

Scientists use little fruit flies from the genus *Drosophila* to study the way genes work. They alter its genetic structure to see how it changes the way the insect grows. Genetic alteration has made this fly grow extra wings. *Drosophila* flies breed very quickly, taking just a few days to reach adulthood, so it is easy to study many generations.

Extra pair of wings

Fruit fly with modified genes

Pest controller

The mongoose is a small carnivore that lives in Asia and Africa. Many species are good at killing snakes, and in some countries they are used as pest controllers, clearing dangerous snakes from houses and gardens. A mongoose can tackle even a cobra, one of the most venomous snakes.

Hidden guard

This Pyrenean mountain dog is one of a breed of large dogs used to protect sheep from wolves, lynxes, and bears in the mountains between France and Spain. It has been bred to be a "dog in sheep's clothing" – its shaggy white fur helps it mingle with the flock, and the sheep soon grow used to it. The dog is ready to attack anything threatening the flock.

Shaggy white fur

Sheep remain calm in dog's presence

Animal friends

People often make room in their families for animals kept as companions. The most popular pets are cats and dogs – there are several hundred million of them, many more than their counterparts surviving in the wild. People also keep other animals as pets, from deadly snakes to tiny insects.

Border collie catches a toy in the air

Many breeds

Each dog breed has certain characteristics. For example, this border collie is intelligent and can follow instructions from its master. Collies are working dogs, commonly used as sheep dogs. The tiny chihuahua breed is the same species as a collie, but is 10 times smaller and was bred to be easy to carry, stroke, and cuddle.

The wolf within

All pet dogs are descended from wild wolves. Dogs and humans are both social species, which makes it easier for them to live together. Wolves began living alongside humans about 15,000 years ago. They scavenged on waste food and, once domesticated, may have teamed up with humans for hunting.

All in the family

Hamsters have pouches in their cheeks that store seeds, a useful feature in these desert rodents as they can go for many days without finding food. These pouches give the hamsters cute rounded faces. In the 1930s, hamsters became fashionable pets. The craze began when a female hamster and her 12 offspring were taken from the wild in Syria and bred as pets.

Skin has blue-grey patches

Creepy pets

Some people like to keep dangerous animals as pets. It was once believed that a tarantula's bite was deadly, and produced dangerous frenzies. The spider was named after a fast-paced Italian dance, the *tarantella*. However, a tarantula's bite is largely harmless to humans.

Mutant creatures

Some breeds of pet are mutants that could not survive in the wild. This strange-looking sphynx cat is descended from a single Canadian cat that was born hairless in 1966. Sphynx cats suffer in cold weather without a covering of hair and would not survive outside a warm house.

Winged companions

Parrots are famous for the way they can copy sounds, such as the ring of a telephone or the flush of a toilet. They even repeat the words people say, which is very enjoyable for their owners. Most parrots are too large to keep in a cage, but budgerigars – little parrots from Australia – make good pets. Parrots are good mimics because, in the wild, they learn a local set of calls by copying older parrots.

Colour of feathers is created by selective breeding

Japanese children play with goldfish

Fish in a bowl

About 1,000 years ago – probably first in China – people began keeping carp as pets. Over the years, people created eye-catching breeds, such as goldfish and koi, which are now found in aquariums across the world. Fish use bright colours to attract mates, and many vibrant species from coral reefs and tropical rivers are also popular pets today.

The wild side

The dingo is one of Australia's most widespread animals. It was introduced to the continent about 4,000 years ago when people brought pet dogs over from Southeast Asia. These dogs escaped and became feral (reverted to a wild state). Now, dingoes living in packs are one of Australia's main predators.

Pests

In the wild there is no such thing as a pest, but humans label some animals "pests" when they damage crops, harm domestic animals, or spread diseases. Humans, meanwhile, have a very large impact on the environment – we turn wild land into fields and cities. While most animals lose areas of their habitat in this process, a few species benefit and thrive in these artificial landscapes.

City slackers

The pigeons living in cities are feral – they are descended from domestic pigeons that were once kept for food or for carrying messages. The wild relatives of pigeons are called rock doves, which roost on steep cliffs. Tall stone buildings make an equally good habitat. City pigeons feed on a diet of waste food, and breed four or five times a year.

Fruit killer

Helix aspersa, or garden snail, is a land snail native to Europe. It is usually seen grazing on leaves in vegetable patches and fruit trees. In the last 150 years, this snail has spread to many other regions of the world by hitching a ride on imported vegetables.

Pest at home

Cockroaches live wherever there is rotting waste, such as leftover food. These pests came from humid African jungles, but have set up home in basements and sewers across the world. Cockroaches are good at staying out of sight. They scavenge in the dark and scuttle quickly into cracks when lights are turned on. They can carry diseases.

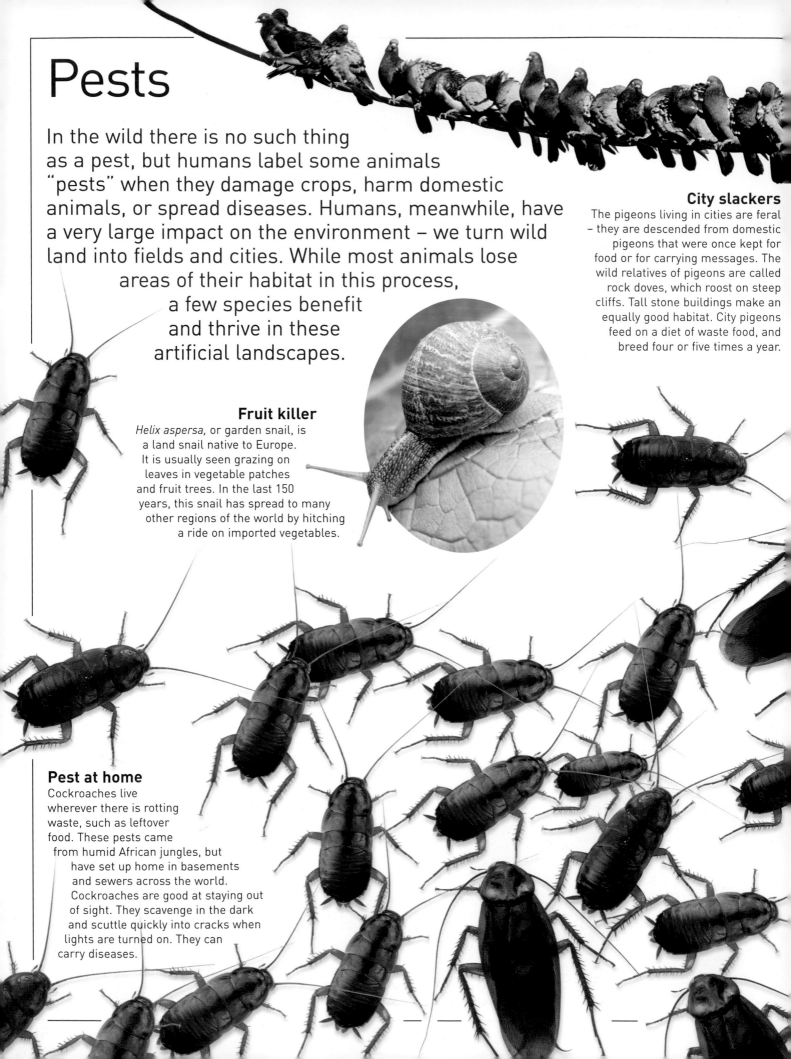

Accidental pest

In the 1930s, giant toads from South America were introduced to Australia, to eat up beetles that were ruining sugar cane crops. These ground-dwelling toads often could not reach the beetles high up in the canes. The plantations were also too dry, so these cane toads left the fields and spread in their millions across eastern Australia. They eventually became a bigger pest themselves – causing a decline in the numbers of many native predators.

Deadly bloodsucker

Female mosquitoes drink the blood of humans and other animals – to get the nutrients they need to grow eggs. When biting an animal, the mosquitoes secrete saliva into the blood of the animal. This saliva may carry germs that can cause deadly diseases, such as yellow fever, elephantiasis, and malaria.

Only the female has the bloodsucking mouthpart

Making a nuisance

Moles are seldom seen, but the hills of soil they produce when digging fresh tunnels ruin a neat lawn. The hills appear in lines as the mole pushes out excavated earth. Moles that dig under trees produce fewer molehills because the tree roots support the burrows.

Small hair on abdomen detects air currents created by an attacker from behind

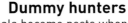
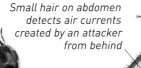

Dummy hunters

Animals become pests when they are taken out of their natural habitats and away from predators that keep their populations from getting too large. However, pests continue to be on the lookout for threats in human settlements. This lifelike model owl keeps crows, mice, and seed-eating birds away from fields and gardens.

Bringer of death

When a pest species arrives in a new area, it can cause devastation. When black rats spread from Asia on board trading ships, fleas living on the rats carried a disease called the plague. The worst outbreak of plague – termed the Black Death – was in the 14th century, when 100 million people were killed. The last major outbreak of the plague in England was in 1665.

Conservation

Human activities affect the natural environment, creating problems for wild animals. Humans continue to remove wild habitats, replacing them with farmland and settlements. Some animals, such as pests or farm animals, thrive under the changes, but most others find life much harder. They may face a shortage of food or places to raise their young, resulting in a drop in their numbers. Many wild animals have also been hunted to extinction by humans.

Pollution
These fish have died after crude oil was spilled into water, filling it with poisons. This is an example of pollution, which is the presence of harmful substances in the environment in unnatural amounts. Pollutants are most often chemicals released into water or air from homes or factories, but can also be excessive heat, or loud noises.

Hunting the hunter
Even this top predator has enemies. People hunt tigers for their skin, to sell body parts as traditional medicines, and sometimes just for sport. Despite their formidable strength, tigers are unable to protect themselves against hunting rifles. In the last 100 years alone, their number have fallen by 95 per cent.

Damaged habitats
One of the ways in which humans endanger animals is by damaging their habitats or even wiping out the habitats completely. The ʻōhiʻa tree is now the only tree from which the ʻiʻiwi bird of Hawaii, with its strange curved beak, can sip nectar. Without this tree, the bird could become extinct.

ʻIʻiwi bird feeding on flowers of an ʻōhiʻa tree

Changing fast
In the Arctic Ocean, walruses rest on ice floes (floating ice) after hunting for shellfish on the sea bed. The area of sea ice in the Arctic has decreased in recent years. Climates and habitats are always changing, but natural changes are slow compared to the rapid changes caused by human activities.

Trade bans

Animals hunted in the wild are often protected by law. A ban on the trade of ivory makes it illegal to sell this elephant tusk anywhere in the world. With this trade ban, the world's governments hoped to reduce the number of elephants killed illegally for their tusks. Since the ban, elephant numbers have been rising.

Tag glued to seal transmits location data to a satellite

Studying animals

Sometimes animal numbers decrease without obvious reason. To understand why, scientists gather data about the environment. This harbour seal lives in an area polluted by an oil spill. It has been fitted with a tag that records where the seal goes to look for fish to eat, and this helps the experts build up a map of which areas of ocean have recovered and which are still polluted.

Walrus uses its tusks to climb on to ice floe

Children watch a penguin parade at Edinburgh Zoo, UK

Learning to care

Protecting endangered animals is called conservation, and one of the most important jobs of a conservationist is teaching people why it is important to look after animals in the wild. Zoos are one place where visitors can find out how they can help threatened animals.

Tourists view animals from safety of a van

Paying for protection

Tourists pay high prices for safaris, where they can see animals in the wild up close. Safari trucks are a common sight in East Africa's national parks. People also visit rainforests hoping to spot a tiger, or take boat trips to see whales. Parks and ecotourism schemes use the money from tourism to protect animals and their natural environments.

61

Animals and myths

Myths and legends from around the globe often feature animals that can do amazing things – not the least of which is the ability to talk to one another. Mythical monsters can have a basis in the natural world. For example, the mythical phoenix has a real-life counterpart – the Tongan megapode bird. The phoenix is a firebird that appears from the hot ashes of its burning mother, while the Tongan megapode bird incubates its eggs in the warm ash of a volcano.

Something fishy
Mermaids are among the most familiar of mythical creatures. They are said to look like a woman with a fish tail instead of legs. Sailors returning from long voyages telling stories of beautiful fish-maidens may have mistaken dugongs or manatees for mermaids. These grazing sea mammals are known as sea cows.

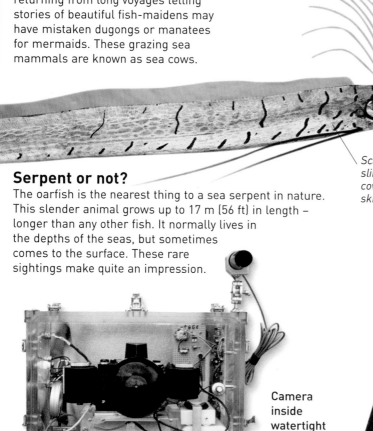

Long crest formed by first few dorsal fin rays

Scaleless, slime-covered skin

Serpent or not?
The oarfish is the nearest thing to a sea serpent in nature. This slender animal grows up to 17 m (56 ft) in length – longer than any other fish. It normally lives in the depths of the seas, but sometimes comes to the surface. These rare sightings make quite an impression.

Camera inside watertight box

Searching for Nessie
This underwater "Creature Camera" was used in the 1970s to look for the world's most famous mythical animal, the Loch Ness Monster. "Nessie" is said to be an immense reptile that lurks in the deep waters of Britain's largest lake. The camera found nothing.

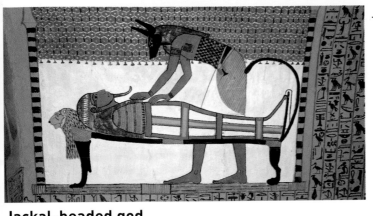

Jackal-headed god

The ancient Egyptians preserved the bodies of dead people as mummies, and were helped on their journey to the afterlife by the God Anubis. Since jackals were probably common in cemeteries, scavenging for human carrion, Anubis' human body and head of a jackal is not so surprising.

Horns of a stag

Dragon statue at Tianhou Temple

Scales of a fish

Flaming pearl said to bestow great powers

Claws of an eagle to

Wing resembles that of a large bird of prey

Birds of thunder

This Native American totem pole is topped with a thunderbird – a flying spirit that was believed to create thunder claps with its wing beats and light up the sky with lightning flashes from its eyes. With its hooked beak, this supernatural creature is most likely modelled on an eagle. Native Americans would have seen, and may have revered, this large bird of prey.

Dragon power

Dragons appear in almost all cultures. They may have been inspired by fossils of giant dinosaurs unearthed by ancient people. In Western traditions, dragons are thought to be brutal beasts that eat people. However, in eastern Asia, dragons are powerful spirits that live in water and under mountains and are usually associated with good luck. This statue of a dragon is dedicated to a sea goddess.

Tusk is a long front tooth grown by males and females

Skull of male narwhal

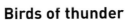

Only one horn

The unicorn is believed be a white deer, or horse, with a single horn on its head. In the Middle Ages, Danish seamen hunted whales called narwhals for their long, spiralled tusks. These often fetched huge sums of money from wealthy collectors who believed they were unicorn horns. The narwhal is a 1-tonne mammal with a 2-m- (6.5-ft-) long spiked tooth sticking out of its head. It may be even more odd-looking than a unicorn.

Record breakers

Among the millions of species that make up the animal kingdom, there are many extraordinary creatures. For example, the blue whale, which is the largest living animal, or the cheetah, which can outrun every other animal on land. Biologists discover new record breakers all the time.

LARGEST COLONY

Argentinian ants
These little South American ants have spread to other parts of the world. A supercolony in Europe runs for 6,000 km (3,730 miles).

Record: Supercolony (billions of ants)

Group: Insects

Habitat: Coast of southern Europe

FASTEST ANIMAL IN WATER

Sailfish
This predatory fish powers through the water with a rapid sweep of its tail and its sword-shaped bill. The sailfish raises its sail-like fin to frighten its prey.

Record: Can reach a speed of 110 kph (68 mph)

Group: Ray-finned fishes

Habitat: Open oceans

LARGEST LAND INVERTEBRATE

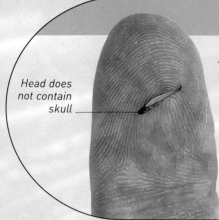

Coconut crab
Also known as the robber crab, this crustacean climbs on palm trees to eat fruits. Its large pincers are strong enough to crack coconuts.

Record: Legspan of 90 cm (35 in)

Group: Crustaceans

Habitat: Tropical islands

HOTTEST HABITAT

Pompeii worm
This sea worm lives in the Pacific Ocean, in the hot water emerging from seafloor volcanic vents. The worm converts chemicals in the water into nutrients.

Record: Can survive at 80 °C (176 °F)

Group: Segmented worms

Habitat: Hydrothermal vents

SMALLEST VERTEBRATE

Head does not contain skull

Australian infantfish
This tiny fish is the smallest animal with a backbone. It lives in muddy swamps made acidic by peat. Being really tiny, the fish can survive in just a tiny puddle of water.

Record: Length of 7.9 mm (0.3 in)

Group: Ray-finned fishes

Habitat: Peat swamps

LOUDEST ANIMAL

Pistol shrimp
The pistol shrimp stuns its prey with a shock wave created by its massive pincer snapping. The sound is so loud it superheats the water.

Record: Can produce sounds at 200 decibels

Group: Crustaceans

Habitat: Coral reefs

SLOWEST FISH

Seahorse
The seahorse can barely swim. A male seahorse spends its entire adult life in the same cubic metre.

Record: 0.001 kph (0.0006 mph)

Group: Ray-finned fishes

Habitat: Seaweed

Tail coiled around seaweed anchors seahorse

FASTEST ANIMAL IN AIR

Peregrine falcon
The peregrine falcon preys on other birds in mid-air, plummeting towards them at high speed from far above. By the time the prey sees the falcon, it is too late.

Record: Max speed of 325 kph (200 mph)

Group: Birds

Habitat: Cliffs

LONGEST PREGNANCY

African elephant
The African elephant's pregnancy is the longest. Its calves weigh 100 kg (220 lb) and must be able to stand and walk soon after birth.

Record: Gestation period of 640 days

Group: Mammals

Habitat: African savannah

STRONGEST ANIMAL

Dung beetle
Dung beetles are able to shift dung balls weighing more than 1,000 times their own weight – the equivalent of a human moving six buses at a time.

Record: Pushes 1,141 times its body weight

Group: Insects

Habitat: Grasslands and forests

STRUCTURE BY A LIVING THING

Australian Great Barrier Reef
Over a period of about 7,000 years, countless generations of coral polyps have built Australia's Great Barrier Reef into a chain of hundreds of reefs and islands.

Record: Length of 2,600 km (1,615 miles)

Group: Cnidarians

Habitat: Warm, shallow waters

Tree of life

Biologists are still figuring out the relationships between different species and those between larger groups of animals. But they know enough to organize animals into a broad tree of life. Closely related animals are clustered together. Sub-groups branch off. Distantly related animals are located far from each other. This tree begins with sponges, the simplest and, perhaps, oldest animal.

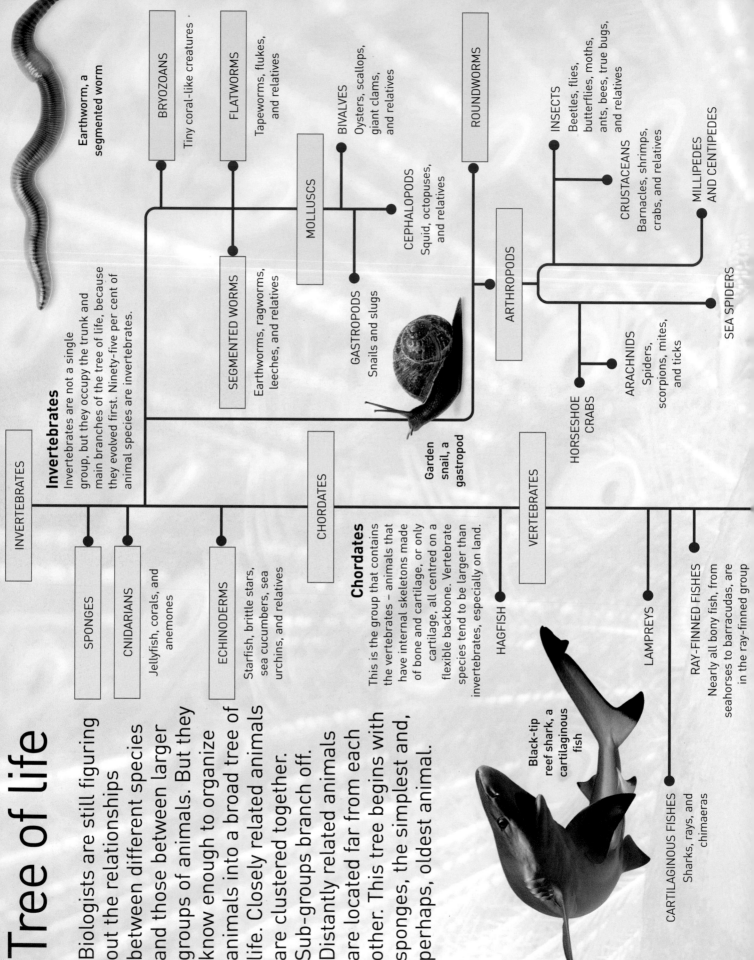

Invertebrates

Invertebrates are not a single group, but they occupy the trunk and main branches of the tree of life, because they evolved first. Ninety-five per cent of animal species are invertebrates.

Earthworm, a segmented worm

INVERTEBRATES

BRYOZOANS
Tiny coral-like creatures

FLATWORMS
Tapeworms, flukes, and relatives

BIVALVES
Oysters, scallops, giant clams, and relatives

MOLLUSCS

CEPHALOPODS
Squid, octopuses, and relatives

ROUNDWORMS

INSECTS
Beetles, flies, butterflies, moths, ants, bees, true bugs, and relatives

CRUSTACEANS
Barnacles, shrimps, crabs, and relatives

MILLIPEDES AND CENTIPEDES

SEGMENTED WORMS
Earthworms, ragworms, leeches, and relatives

GASTROPODS
Snails and slugs

ARTHROPODS

ARACHNIDS
Spiders, scorpions, mites, and ticks

HORSESHOE CRABS

SEA SPIDERS

Garden snail, a gastropod

SPONGES

CNIDARIANS
Jellyfish, corals, and anemones

ECHINODERMS
Starfish, brittle stars, sea cucumbers, sea urchins, and relatives

CHORDATES

Chordates

This is the group that contains the vertebrates – animals that have internal skeletons made of bone and cartilage, or only cartilage, all centred on a flexible backbone. Vertebrate species tend to be larger than invertebrates, especially on land.

VERTEBRATES

HAGFISH

LAMPREYS

RAY-FINNED FISHES
Nearly all bony fish, from seahorses to barracudas, are in the ray-finned group

Black-tip reef shark, a cartilaginous fish

CARTILAGINOUS FISHES
Sharks, rays, and chimaeras

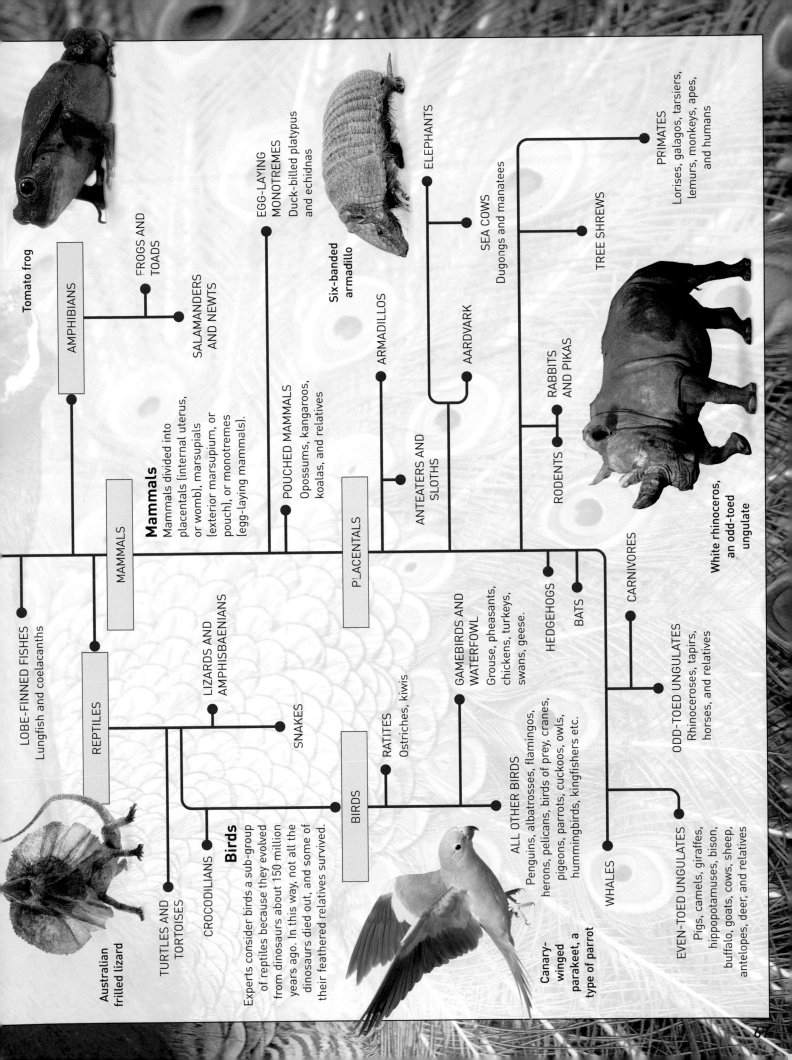

Tomato frog

Australian
frilled lizard

AMPHIBIANS

FROGS AND
TOADS

SALAMANDERS
AND NEWTS

EGG-LAYING
MONOTREMES
Duck-billed platypus
and echidnas

Six-banded
armadillo

ELEPHANTS

SEA COWS
Dugongs and manatees

PRIMATES
Lorises, galagos, tarsiers,
lemurs, monkeys, apes,
and humans

TREE SHREWS

AARDVARK

ARMADILLOS

Mammals
Mammals divided into
placentals (internal uterus,
or womb), marsupials
(exterior marsupium, or
pouch), or monotremes
(egg-laying mammals).

MAMMALS

POUCHED MAMMALS
Opossums, kangaroos,
koalas, and relatives

ANTEATERS AND
SLOTHS

RABBITS
AND PIKAS

PLACENTALS

RODENTS

White rhinoceros,
an odd-toed
ungulate

LOBE-FINNED FISHES
Lungfish and coelacanths

LIZARDS AND
AMPHISBAENIANS

SNAKES

HEDGEHOGS

BATS

CARNIVORES

REPTILES

TURTLES AND
TORTOISES

CROCODILIANS

Birds

Experts consider birds a sub-group
of reptiles because they evolved
from dinosaurs about 150 million
years ago. In this way, not all the
dinosaurs died out, and some of
their feathered relatives survived.

GAMEBIRDS AND
WATERFOWL
Grouse, pheasants,
chickens, turkeys,
swans, geese.

ODD-TOED UNGULATES
Rhinoceroses, tapirs,
horses, and relatives

BIRDS

RATITES
Ostriches, kiwis

ALL OTHER BIRDS
Penguins, albatrosses, flamingos,
herons, pelicans, birds of prey, cranes,
pigeons, parrots, cuckoos, owls,
hummingbirds, kingfishers etc.

WHALES

**Canary-
winged
parakeet, a
type of parrot**

EVEN-TOED UNGULATES
Pigs, camels, giraffes,
hippopotamuses, bison,
buffalo, goats, cows, sheep,
antelopes, deer, and relatives

Animal watch

Blue tits are attracted to a nut-filled feeder

Setting the scene

Animals are predictable and this works to a watcher's advantage. All animals need to eat and they often return to known feeding sites. For example, grizzly bears in Alaska gather near rivers in the autumn to catch salmon migrating upstream. People also attract animals, such as blue tits, to a viewing spot by providing food.

Observing animals requires a bit of skill and a lot of patience. Getting a good look at an animal in its natural habitat can be quite difficult. Wild animals are wary of anything unusual, but knowing when and where an animal will appear is crucial to studying them in the wild.

Magnifying glass helps study small invertebrates closely

A compact, weight-saving model

Notebook for sketching animals and noting location, time, and weather conditions of sightings

A grizzly bear catches a fish in Alaska

Binoculars allow watchers to see details at a distance

Getting ready

Wildlife watchers carry equipment for finding and viewing animals, recording the animals in their natural habitats, and perhaps even capturing a few. Nature lovers spend a lot of time outdoors in all kinds of weather. They need warm and dry clothing, that does not make rustling sounds, in muted colours to avoid standing out.

Walking boots keep feet warm and dry, and are comfortable on long hikes

Sun hat provides shade and also breaks up the tell-tale shape of the head

Large grips reduce chances of slipping in mud and on loose stones

FOLLOWING THE SEASONS

As the weather of a region changes with the seasons, so does the behaviour of animals living there. A good wildlife watcher will know where a species is likely to be at each time of year. For example, they do not look for European hedgehogs in winter but only in summer, when the ball-shaped nests of these animals can be seen in bushes and thickets.

These common cranes have arrived in northern Europe in early summer to breed. They perform distinctive courtship displays to attract mates.

This flock of pink-footed geese is leaving Greenland in autumn for Europe, where many birdwatchers travel to watch them arrive.

Hide has a camouflage pattern to help it blend in with surroundings

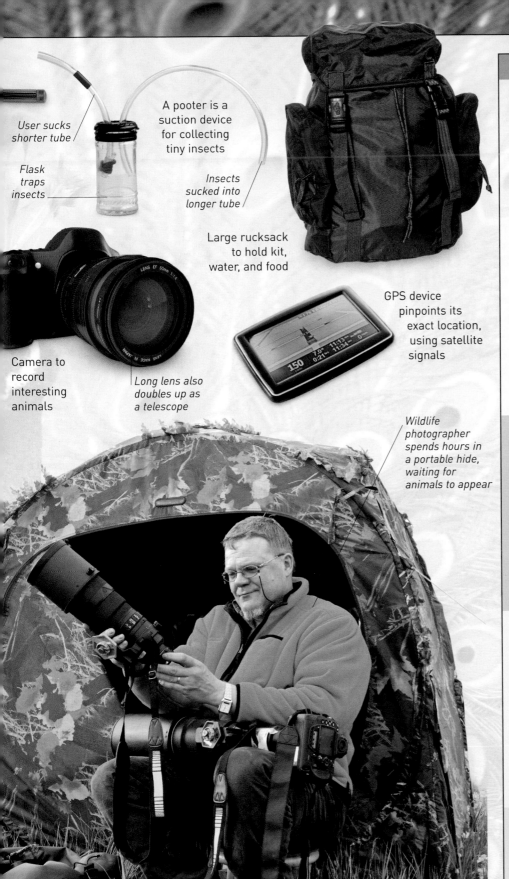

User sucks shorter tube

Flask traps insects

A pooter is a suction device for collecting tiny insects

Insects sucked into longer tube

Large rucksack to hold kit, water, and food

Camera to record interesting animals

Long lens also doubles up as a telescope

GPS device pinpoints its exact location, using satellite signals

Wildlife photographer spends hours in a portable hide, waiting for animals to appear

READING THE SIGNS

Wildlife experts can find animals from the signs they leave behind. Large animals leave distinctive footprints in snow and mud, as well as broken twigs and flattened plants. Trackers keep an eye out for the signs that animals leave for each other, such as dung piles, smelly scents, and scratches in trees.

These marks are left by a red deer, known as an elk in North America, chewing on bark during winter. Fresh marks show that the deer may be nearby.

A black bear marks its territory by gouging deep scratches in soft tree bark with its claws and teeth. The height of the mark shows how tall the bear is.

This tree has been gnawed by a beaver as it collects logs for constructing its dam. This rodent will have dug a channel nearby leading to its pool.

These holes were made by a woodpecker looking for wood-boring insects under the bark. The noise made by this chiselling gives away the bird's position.

Glossary

ALGAE Organisms that photosynthesize like a plant, but are mostly single-celled. Algae often live in water or damp places.

AQUATIC To do with water. Aquatic animals spend most of their time in water.

ARTERY A blood vessel that carries oxygen-rich blood from the heart to other body organs.

BACTERIA Tiny, single-celled organisms that are not plant, animal, or fungus. Bacterial cells are at least 100 times smaller than an animal cell. Most bacteria are harmless, but some cause disease.

BRACKISH Water that is partly salty and partly fresh. Brackish water is found in coastal swamps and river mouths where fresh water mixes with sea water.

Chameleon, an ectotherm

BIOLUMINESCENCE Ability of some animals to produce light using chemicals or specialized bacteria in their bodies. Bioluminescent animals generally live in the dark.

CARBON DIOXIDE A gas produced as a waste product by animals when they extract energy by processing sugars and other foods in their bodies. Animals take in oxygen and give out carbon dioxide when they breathe.

CARNIVORE An animal that mostly eats meat – the flesh of other animals. Carnivores are generally predators, often killing animals that they eat.

CHITIN A tough material in the outer body coverings of many invertebrates.

CHROMOSOME A microscopic structure in the cells of all animals that is used as a frame around which long strands of DNA are coiled.

COLD-BLOODED Also known as ectothermic, a cold-blooded animal is one that cannot maintain a constant body temperature. Instead, its body temperature varies with the environmental conditions.

CORPSE The body of a dead animal.

DNA Short for deoxyribonucleic acid, DNA is a complex chemical formed from a chain of four chemical units, or bases. The genetic code of an animal is stored in the way these four bases are ordered in its DNA chains.

Brown fungus growing on log

DORSAL FIN The fin on the back of an aquatic animal, such as a shark or a dolphin. The fin stops the animal from rolling as it swims.

ECTOTHERM A cold-blooded animal. *Ecto* means "outside" and *therm* is "heat" – an ectotherm uses outside heat.

ENDOTHERM A warm-blooded animal. *Endo* means "inside"; an endotherm uses its body heat to stay warm.

ENZYME A protein chemical with a specific job to do in an animal's body. Digestive enzymes break up certain foods into simpler ingredients, while other enzymes copy DNA. An enzyme's special shape helps it perform its task.

EVOLUTION A process by which organisms change over a period of time, and across many generations, as they adapt to changes in the environment. New species are often formed in this process.

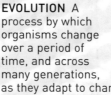

Clownfish, a hermaphrodite – changes from male to female

EXTINCT A species that has died out.

FUNGUS An organism that is neither an animal nor a plant. A fungus, such as a mushroom, grows into its food and digests it externally.

GENE A strand of DNA that carries the instructions for a characteristic of an organism – such as the colour of a bird's feathers, or the shape of its wings.

GILL The organ used by many aquatic animals to absorb oxygen from water and give out carbon dioxide.

GIZZARD A muscular part of a bird's gut used to grind food.

HABITAT The place where an animal lives.

Toucan's bill contains keratin

HERBIVORE An animal that only eats plant food. It may eat leaves (folivore), fruits (frugivore), seeds (granivore), sap and juices (exudivore), or roots (radicivore).

HERMAPHRODITE An animal that has both male and female sex organs. Some hermaphrodites start life as one sex and change into the other as they grow. Other hermaphrodites have both sets of sex organs at the same time.

HYBRID A cross between two species or breeds. A mule is a hybrid of a horse and a donkey, while a mongrel is a hybrid between dog breeds.

INSULATOR A substance that stops heat escaping from an animal's body, keeping it warm. Blubber, feathers, and hair are the common insulators found in animals.

INVERTEBRATE Any animal that is not a member of the phylum Chordata. Most of the world's animals are invertebrates.

KERATIN A flexible protein present in the external body features of vertebrates, such as hair, feathers, claws, scales, horn sheaths, and fingernails.

KLEPTOPARASITE An animal that survives by stealing food from another hunter, generally of a different species.

LARVA The young form of an insect or other invertebrate that looks different to the adult form and also lives in a different way. A caterpillar is an example of a larva.

LIFT FORCE The force that pushes a flying animal off the ground.

MEMBRANE A thin layer or barrier that may allow some substances to pass through.

MICROSCOPIC When something is too small to see with the naked eye. A microscope is used to observe it.

NUTRIENTS The useful parts of food, such as sugars, proteins, fats, oils, vitamins, and minerals. An animal's digestive system extracts these from food.

NYMPH An early stage of development of an insect or other invertebrate that generally looks and lives in the same way as the organism's adult form.

OXYGEN A substance used by an animal's body in chemical reactions that release energy from sugars and other foods. It is taken in by breathing in air or absorbing it from water.

PARASITE An animal that lives on or in another animal of a different species.

Diving beetle nymph

PHYLUM The largest grouping used to organize, or classify, life. There are dozens of animal phyla. Some of the main ones are Arthropoda (insects and crabs), Mollusca (snails and squid), and Chordata (vertebrates).

PIGMENTS Chemicals that give colour to an organism. Giving colour may be the main function of the pigment or the coloration may be incidental. For example, the pigments in the eye are used as light detectors.

PREDATOR An animal that hunts and kills other animals for food.

PROTEIN A complex chemical found in all life forms, but most prominently in animals. Proteins help build body parts. Enzymes are examples of proteins.

SALIVA The liquid produced by salivary glands in the mouth of an animal to moisten food, making it easier to swallow and digest.

SCUTE An armoured plate of bone covered in skin or horny keratin. A turtle shell is made up of interlocking scutes, while a crocodile's body is protected by ridges of scutes.

SPECIES A group of animals that look the same and live in the same way, and are also able to breed with each other to produce fertile offspring that will be able to reproduce themselves.

SYMBIOSIS A partnership between two animals of different species that live with each other. In most cases, each animal provides a service or benefit to the other in the relationship.

TERRITORY An area of land or water defended by an animal. Territory is used as a feeding space or as an area for mates to live and unwanted members of the same species are driven away.

TETRAPOD A vertebrate with four limbs.

URINE The liquid waste of mammals and other animals. While dung, or faeces, is the undigested materials in food, urine is the waste removed from the blood and body tissues.

VEIN A blood vessel that carries oxygen-poor blood from the body organs towards the heart.

Turtle shell contains scutes

VENOM Poison that is produced by an animal and injected into another by a bite, scratch, or sting. Venom is used in hunting as well as in defence.

VERTEBRATE An animal with a backbone – a set of small vertebrae that connect to form a flexible spine. The vertebrate groups are fish, amphibians, reptiles, birds, and mammals.

WARM-BLOODED Also known as endothermic, a warm-blooded animal is one that controls its body temperature internally, using a lot of energy to heat or cool its body, so it stays at more or less the same temperature whatever the weather conditions at that time.

Leopard, a predator, with its kill

Index
ABC

Acknowledgements

Dorling Kindersley would like to thank: Caitlin Doyle for proofreading; Dr Laurence Errington for the index; Aanchal Awasthi, Honlung Zach Ragui, and Nitu Singh for design assistance; and Dan Green for text editing.

The publishers would also like to thank the following for their kind permission to reproduce their photographs:
(Key: a-above; b-below/bottom; c-centre; f-far; l-left; r-right; t-top)

Alamy Images: Amazon-Images 23tr, CML Images 59br, Mark Conlin / VWPICS / Visual&Written SL 42bl, Stephen Dalton / Photoshot Holdings Ltd 39tr, Chris Mattison 32tr, Mauritius images GmbH 32b, MicroScan / Phototake Inc. 12br, Todd Mintz 42crb, Mira 26tl, Richard Mittleman / Gon2Foto 11br, V. Muthuraman / SuperStock 36clb, NaturePics 64cra, Matthew Oldfield 24br, Clément Philippe / Arterra Picture Library 69crb, Bjorn Svensson / Science Photo Library 69br, Duncan Usher 48–49bc, Dave Watts 13cr, 17ca; **Ardea:** Steve Downer 27bl, Ferrero-Labat 22–23c, François Gohier 48bl, Stefan Meyers 30cra; **Corbis:** Hinrich Baesemann / DPA 30-31b, Hal Beral 9tr, Carolina Biological / Visuals Unlimited 10cla, Nigel Cattlin / Visuals Unlimited 15clb, Ralph Clevenger 42–43, Dr John D. Cunningham / Visuals Unlimited 69cr, Mark Downey 2bc, 24tl, Macduff Everton 53cla, Michael & Patricia Fogden 18–19, 36bl, Stephen Frink 10b, Tim Graham 68br, James Hager / Robert Harding World Imagery 23c, Dave

Hamman / Gallo Images 55crb, Martin Harvey 37br, Martin Harvey / Gallo Images 22bl, Eric & David Hosking 4tl, 48cl, Jason Isley - Scubazoo / Science Faction 42cl, Wolfgang Kaehler 28br, Karen Kasmauski / Science Faction 61tr, Thomas Kitchin & Victoria Hurst / First Light 13br, Peter Kneffel / DPA 54tl, Stephen J. Krasemann / All Canada Photos 34tl, Frans Lanting 4bl, 31cl, 33br, 60bc, Frans Lemmens 49cra, Wayne Lynch / All Canada Photos 31cb, John E. Marriott / All Canada Photos 31tr, Dan McCoy - Rainbow / Science Faction 50cla, Joe McDonald 11clb, 38cl, 68cl, Tim Mckulka / UNMIS / Reuters 52–53, Dong Naide / Xinhua Press 53tr, David A. Northcott 6tl, Michael Redmer / Visuals Unlimited 6bc (plethodon jordani), 9tl, Bryan Reynolds / Science Faction 9fcra (leeches), David Scharf / Science Faction 55cl, Shoot 60tl, David Spears / Clouds Hill Imaging Ltd. 65tc, Keren Su 55tl, Jeff Vanuga 58t, Carlos Villoch / Specialist Stock 26–27, Visuals Unlimited 7br, 44tl, Stuart Westmorland 8clb, 11tr, Ralph White 62bl, Lawson Wood 27br, Norbert Wu / Science Faction 20bl, 47c; **Dorling Kindersley:** ESPL - modelmaker 50r, Exmoor Zoo, Devon 15cra (Azara's Agouti), Hunterian Museum (University of Glasgow) 4cr, 17tr, Trustees of the National Museums Of Scotland 17cla, Natural History Museum, London 4br (larger cockroach), 8tr, 12fbr, 13tl, 16cra, 44br, 58br (two larger coackroaches), 58fcrb (larger cockroach), 59c (larger cockroach), 68ftr, Based on a photo by David Robinson / The Open University 33cla, Rough Guides 50bl, 51br, 61crb, Stanley Park,

Totem Park, Vancouver, British Columbia 2l, 63r, University College, London 51l, Whipsnade Zoo, Bedfordshire Barrie Watts 66ca, 67cra, Jerry Young 4tr, 4cra, 10-11tc, 24cra, 37ca, 56cla, 67tl; **FLPA:** Ingo Arndt / Minden Pictures 37tr, Flip De Nooyer / Minden 68bc, Michael Durham / Minden Pictures 19cra (leeches), Suzi Eszterhas / Minden Pictures 47br, John Holmes 30-31tc, Donald M. Jones / Minden Pictures 69cra, Mark Moffett / Minden Pictures 29tr, Jurgen & Christine Sohns 35tr, Konrad Wothe / Minden Pictures 45cr, 65cla, Norbert Wu / Minden Pictures 47clb; **Fotolia:** Eric Isselee 60cl; **Getty Images:** AFP 64bl, Gerry Bishop / Visuals Unlimited 46br, Tom Brakefield - The Stock Connection / Science Faction 15br, The Bridgeman Art Library 57cr, Stephen Dalton / Minden Pictures 29br, George Day / Gallo Images 8tl, David Doubilet / National Geographic 8-9bc, Georgette Douwma / Photographer's Choice 27br, Richard du Toit / Gallo Images 47tr, Guy Edwardes / The Image Bank 59tl, Eurasia / Robert Harding World Imagery 62-63bc, George Grall / National Geographic 18clb, Louis-Laurent Grandadam / The Image Bank 55b, Jamie Grill 69ca, Henry Guttmann / Hulton Archive 15tl, Hulton Archive 59bl, David Maitland 44cra, Joe McDonald / Visuals Unlimited 46-47, Bruno Morandi / The Image Bank 20tl, Marwan Naamani / AFP 33tr, Piotr Naskrecki / Minden Pictures 33cb, Iztok Noc / Photodisc 56-57, Radius Images 65br, 71cra, David Silverman 23br, Keren Su 7tr, U.S. Navy 54bl, Mario Vazquez / AFP 43tr, Gary Vestal / Photographer's Choice 7l, 25b, Alex Wild / Visuals Unlimited, Inc. 65cly; **imagequestmarine.com:** 64br; **NASA:** GSFC / Craig Mayhew &Robert Simmon 51t; **naturepl. com:** Chris Gomersall 41tc, Rolf Nussbaumer 45l, Andy Rouse 36r, Kim Taylor 25tr, 38b (dragonflies), Dave Watts 40tc, 40tr, Wild

Wonders of Europe / Rautiainen 69bl; **Photolibrary:** Kathie Atkinson / Oxford Scientific (OSF) 40clb, Stefan Auth / Imagebroker.net 54br, Paulo de Oliveira / Oxford Scientific (OSF) 10cra, 62cla, David B. Fleetham / Oxford Scientific (OSF) 27cr, François Gilson / Bios 40bl, jspix jspix / Imagebroker.net 12tr, Steven Kazlowski / Alaskastock 60-61c, Morales Morales / Age fotostock 64clb, Rolf Nussbaumer / Imagebroker.net 21clb, Frank Parker / Age fotostock 35 (main image), Jean-Paul Chatagnon / Bios 49tr, Gerhard Schultz / Oxford Scientific (OSF) 40crb, Gerhard Schulz / Bios 41crb, M. Varesvuo 20-21tc; **Science Photo Library:** Susumu Nishinaga 12bc, Power & Syred 21tl, 46tr, D. Roberts 39br, Volker Steger 21crb, 21fcrb; **SuperStock:** Minden Pictures 33cla.

Wall Chart images: **Corbis:** Peter Kneffel / DPA (crb/rescue dog), Frans Lanting (cra/penguin), Norbert Wu / Science Faction (crb/spotted shrimp goby); **Dorling Kindersley:** Natural History Museum, London (br/larger cockroach); **Getty Images:** Georgette Douwma / Photographer's Choice (fcra/fish), Gary Vestal / Photographer's Choice (c); **Photolibrary:** jspix jspix / Imagebroker.net (tl/macaw).

Jacket images: Front: **Ardea:** M. Watson (main image); **Dorling Kindersley:** Natural History Museum, London tr/(skull); **Getty Images:** Don Farrall / Photographer's Choice tc/(butterfly); naturepl.com: Nick Garbutt ftr; *Back:* **Photolibrary:** Watt Jim / Pacific Stock bl, jspix jspix / Imagebroker.net tl.

All other images © Dorling Kindersley
For further information see: www.dkimages.com